I0532439

Finding Joy in The Grief Cycle

Your guide to navigating grief

by Becky Beck

SCAN FOR BOOK CLUB VIDEOS

PRAISE FOR FINDING JOY IN THE GRIEF CYCLE

I enjoyed, so much, reading Becky Beck's latest book, *Finding Joy in The Grief Cycle*. It has now been 22 years since we lost our first born daughter, at age 32, in the prime of her life. She had a very successful career, was engaged to be married, and seemed happier than she had ever been, but this beautiful life was snuffed out by a drunk driver. For more than three years I was full of hate for the young man who seemingly, without remorse or thought, chose to drive while intoxicated, killing our daughter. I wish I had this book back in 2001 as I was stuck in anger, depression, and denial. There are so many thoughts and feelings that this book ignites or will ignite in the reader, even when tragedy has numbed their senses. Even after 22 years, I experienced many tears as I read this book. Becky brings the Savior and His teachings to life, giving praise and adoration where it belongs. She has a special talent to put into words such deep and meaningful emotions and thoughts. -Ken

Finding Joy in The Grief Cycle is short, thought provoking, and to the point. It is raw and real, yet full of hope. Each chapter contains helpful questions to ponder and invitations to act on to facilitate moving forward through the grief cycle. The principles discussed are based on scripture and beautifully express how anyone can invite Jesus into their grief, ultimately turning mourning and lamentation into joy through Him. -Sally

I needed the chapter on mourning so much. Just last night and this morning I found myself grieving the loss of my husband again. I thought I would be doing better by now, but I began grieving all over again, shedding many tears. After reading I understand why my nights and mornings are still really hard. -Marsha

Finding Joy in The Grief Cycle is a very insightful look into dealing with one of the inevitable moments in life: the death of a loved one. As I've had the opportunity to bury both of my parents, my brother-in-law and my father-in-law I wish this well defined process of mourning and grief would have been available a few years ago. I highly recommend a serious reading and study of The Grief Cycle process to help make this time in our lives much easier for us to cope, heal, recover, and celebrate the lives of our loved ones. -Lloyd

What you teach about turning everything over to the Lord and trusting Him really resonated with me. I remember turning to the Lord and saying "Heavenly Father, I know you are there to give me strength and comfort, and with You there I can get through this." I said this prayer as I went through my husband's cancer before he passed, and then again as my daughter was ill, before she too passed away. "Believing" that He is there gets me through some of my hardest times. Could not do this without Him. -Patti

Thank you so much for writing this book to help us souls that might need a plan to navigate through this lifelong journey. I find myself doing projects to distract me from my grief. I'm sure my mourning is coming. -Gloria

We celebrated our grandsons this past week as a family. There was great healing and that bonding has been a beautiful blessing. We have so many wonderful memories to be thankful for. My heart is full of gratitude for the six weeks they stayed with us last summer. Some days it is so hard to write my feelings. I will certainly add the evening and morning time to acknowledge my grief in positive ways. I feel I can face the coming days more cheerfully as I live in The Grief Cycle. Thank you! -LaVon

Thank you for reminding me that it is okay to feel and that I can breathe my way through painful triggers. I'm more of a "bury it until you can't bury it any more" kind of person. It becomes a vicious cycle. I will practice this breathing technique to help me move through my emotions of grief. And, yes, the Lord is in the details! -Gail

When you taught about making space to mourn, it made a lot of sense to me. I didn't start to heal emotionally after losing my grandmothers until I had a space to mourn. -Brianon

Dedicated to my youngest son, Baby Kevin, who taught me the beauty of the worth of a soul. And to my dad, Papa Tom, who taught me what it means to endure to the end. And to my Savior, Jesus Christ, who has healed my broken heart and shown me how to find joy in my grief.

CONTENTS

–·–

INTRODUCTION

DOORWAYS

I didn't expect to find truth in the movie theater. My nine-year-old dad and his five siblings went to a lot of movies with their mom in the weeks and months following their dad's death from brain cancer at age 46. She said it was a way to escape the grief for a bit. A chance to get lost in someone else's story, and hopefully laugh a little. I've done that too, not just to take a break from grief, but movies help me be present and give me a welcome break from my overactive mind.

Last summer my husband and I took our two youngest daughters to see Disney's new *Haunted Mansion* movie. We love the Haunted Mansion ride in Disneyland and the original movie with Eddie Murphy. We expected the second movie to be similar to the first, and it was. But I was not expecting the movie to be about grief. The movie screen blurred and my eyes filled with tears as Madame Leota spoke the words, "Even grief can be a doorway to joy if one is willing to walk through it." The truthfulness of those words pierced my heart.

The thing is, we never know, as we walk through the various doorways of life, how many of them ultimately lead to the door that says, "The Grief House, Visitors Welcome."

I walked through one of those doorways shortly after our daughter Gracie was born. I have always felt heaven close with each of our newborns, but I'll never forget the experience I had when Gracie was just a few weeks old. I was in our living room and suddenly had an overwhelming feeling that we had another son waiting to join our family. The impression was so strong it was as if his spirit was in the room with me.

Gracie was our fifth child. I had finally got the hang of being a mama, and the idea of one more boy, bringing the head count to an even three girls and three boys, sounded like a great plan. I could picture him, but unlike his brothers, I imagined that he would take more after his daddy, with blonde hair and blue eyes.

I was so excited to have another son and willingly walked through another doorway a couple of years later when we began trying to get pregnant.

I find it interesting that when God gives us a glimpse into our future, we can be quick to fill in the rest of the story leading up to it. At least that's how the perpetual planner in me operates. I soon found that God's plan was a completely different story. Instead of our son joining us two or three years after Gracie, it took seven years of waiting. Plot twist: God sent us two more daughters after Gracie, which both tried my faith and patience, and also brought me blessings I didn't know I needed. With every pregnancy, I fully expected it to be the son whose presence I had felt so strongly. When I learned otherwise, I figured the next baby would be our son.

Jackson (17), Emmy (15), Dakota (13), Kloe (10), Gracie (7), Janie (3), and Lilly (10 months), my husband Kevin and I were elated to learn through an ultrasound on my fortieth birthday, that our boy was finally on his way. We couldn't wait to meet him. Plot twist: a couple weeks later, at twenty weeks pregnant, our son was diagnosed with Trisomy 13, a fetal anomaly "incompatible with life." That certainly DID NOT align with my plan. I was devastated. The entire family was devastated. The doctors said the baby could pass away at any time and would most likely not make it to full term.

With my plan shattered, there were only two things I knew to do. I opened my hands, reluctantly at first, and let go. I let go of the way I thought our story should unfold. Then I turned to God in humility and faith, trusting in His plan for our son. And since I didn't know how long I would have my baby with me, I decided to embrace every day he was inside me. I didn't stop at the doorway of The Grief House; I opened the door and walked right in.

We named him right away, Kevin David, after his father and grandfather. I took him with me on trips, tucked inside me where I could keep him alive with my own healthy body. Got to know him as I felt of his perfect spirit, and introduced him to family and friends. Held him close inside as I rocked him. Took him to the temple with me so his body could be blessed through mine. And rejoiced with every hiccup, punch, kick, and roll.

I did my best to grieve with grace and hope. As I explored my house of grief, the Lord never left me. Jesus was there to comfort me during my sleepless nights, disappointing doctor visits, and waves of overwhelming sorrow. Jesus was at my side as I said goodbye to my son. Plot twist: somehow, Christ turned the most difficult and painful days of my life into a sacred and beautiful experience, not just for me, but for our whole family. And the joy we felt in the midst of it all was the most unexpected gift from a loving Father in Heaven.

In my previous memoir, *Too Perfect for This Life*, I share my love for motherhood and our story of walking through the doorway of anticipatory grief. Despite all its painful rooms and stairs with steep climbs, there were many hope-filled hallways and great big windows, streaming in so much love and light along the way. I found joy in each corner of every room. In this book I share a framework to help you take your first step through the doorway of *your* grief house, find comfort in this new home, and have the courage to explore every room until your grief lightens and you're ready to build a new house.

Whether you are grieving the loss of someone you love, or any type of life experience that didn't go as planned, stepping into The Grief Cycle will guide and support you through your grief. I am so sorry for your loss, but I rejoice in the journey that awaits you as you turn to Christ and accept the invitation He gives in Matthew 11:28: "Come unto me, all ye that are heavy laden, and I will give you rest." He has done this for me, and He can do it for you too, if you are willing to walk through the doorway of grief.

Take your time as you make your way through this book. Each chapter will offer ideas for you to consider and simple things you can do to find peace, healing, and joy as you learn to grieve within *The Grief Cycle*.

At the end of each chapter you'll notice a "Questions to Ponder" section. These questions can be worked through in a book club discussion, or with a friend walking the same path. I invite you to think and pray about the questions, then if you like, take a moment to journal your response. This simple exercise will help you turn to your Savior, so He can take you by the hand and be your personal guide through your grief journey. You can do this – and you too may find joy, even in your grief journey.

Check out the
Book Club Videos
⟶

1

———

JUST BREATHE

"AND THE LORD GOD FORMED MAN OF THE DUST OF THE GROUND, AND BREATHED INTO HIS NOSTRILS THE BREATH OF LIFE; AND MAN BECAME A LIVING SOUL." GENESIS 2:7

"You have to breathe, Beck," my husband kept repeating as I gripped the hospital bed rails, trying my best to make it through another contraction. Nothing was going as *planned*. I'm a really good *planner* and I'd *planned* well for the birth of our eighth child, who'd miraculously made it to 37 weeks, despite all the abnormalities throughout his little body. With seven other births over the past 18 years, I was a pro when it came to delivering babies. In the days and weeks leading up to my deliveries, I'm always in the early stages of labor. By the time I walk into the delivery room I'm usually dilated to a 4 (out of 10). I've got a system: epidural anesthesia, the doctor breaks my water, and within an hour or so, it's go time. Given my history, I assumed we'd be delivering our son right around dinner time. You would think, after experiencing four months of nothing going as planned, I would have surrendered the day of my son's birth as well. But I didn't, and instead, gripped hard to my birth plan.

What I had not planned for was the pitocin, a drug to induce labor, which my doctor included in her plan. I didn't need pitocin. We arrived at the hospital that morning around 8 a.m. Just me and my husband. I changed into the pink polka dot gown I brought from home and was hooked up to the IV within the hour. It wasn't long before the steady drip of pitocin took over, and suddenly I was no longer in control. By noon I was dilated to 8½. Minutes later a 9. At that point I knew there was no turning back, and obviously, there would be no epidural. There was also no husband. He too thought we would be having a baby around dinner time. He was outside, trying to get cell service to let the birth photographer know to come sooner. He returned to my side just as the doctor was prepping me for delivery. I was holding my breath as the contractions intensified. Between contractions I remember saying to the nurses, "I didn't prepare for this, I've never taken a lamaze class,[1] I don't even know how to breathe." I had taken for granted my body's ability to breathe automatically for the last forty years. I also assumed I would have an epidural, allowing me to sail through delivery without any pain. Struggling to breathe through intense pain,

---

1. Relating to a method of childbirth involving exercises and breathing control to give pain relief without drugs.

mingled with some fear of the unknown, was a new experience for me. Listening to my husband's voice, "You have to breathe Beck, you have to breathe...", helped me stay focused and present as I tried to breathe through the pain of each contraction. At 12:26 p.m. our son, Kevin Jr. was born—or Baby Kevin, as everyone affectionately called him. A few moments later, he miraculously took his first breath.

Baby Kevin had been diagnosed with Trisomy 13 at twenty weeks (more on this later.) It was a miracle he was born alive. He began crying shortly after he was born—another miracle. He cried for around ten minutes. I wondered if he was as sad to leave us as we were to let him go.

Life is not for the faint of heart. Very few of us make it through being a human without the experience of being beaten down by grief. Add financial struggles, health challenges, betrayal, loneliness, disappointment, trauma, and abuse. Even just one or two of those can become a recipe for triggering the fight, flight, or freeze response in our bodies. And when that happens, we unknowingly hold our breath and forget to breathe. Thank goodness God wired us to breathe automatically, or we'd all live much shorter lives.

As I prepared to write this book, I spent months poring over old journals and blog posts, revisiting my experience with grieving the loss of my son and later my father. At times I was overcome with emotion. Many of my past grief triggers resurfaced. Maybe the same will apply to you as you continue reading.

I'll never forget my first major trigger a couple of weeks after my son died. My grief was raw and my emotions were all over the place. As long as I was with Kevin I could manage, and he stayed by my side – until he and the boys left town for a fishing trip one weekend. I decided to brave going to church with the girls. I figured I was safe because we would be visiting my aunt's congregation, where I didn't know anyone except for a few family members. No one else knew about my loss. I was too emotional to talk about it. I knew my home congregation would wrap me right up in their arms, but I wasn't ready to add more emotion to my already fragile heart.

We found a seat in the chapel. So far so good. And then my Aunt Judy, the greatest organist of all time, began to play the opening hymn, "How Firm a Foundation." That song gave me comfort throughout my pregnancy because it is all about Jesus and how we don't need to fear because He is always with us. My tears began to fall as the congregation sang, "Fear not, I am with thee; oh be not dismayed, For I am thy God and will still give thee aid. I'll strengthen thee, help thee, and cause thee to stand, Upheld by my righteous, omnipotent hand."[2]

---

2. https://www.churchofjesuschrist.org/music/library/hymns/how-firm-a-foundation?lang=eng

I couldn't sing as I wept. I could barely breathe. I wanted to run, but instead I sat there, feeling all my feelings, forcing myself to breathe. By the time the song ended I was okay.

My triggers were like that person you don't invite to the party that shows up anyway. Over time, I got used to the triggers, and eventually the intensity and frequency diminished. Today I see triggers as simply reminders. They can be painful, or they can be sweet, and sometimes both. Today, most of my triggers revolving around my son lean towards the sweet kind; mixed in are some painful reminders. At times, they're bittersweet. Your triggers may be more painful and frequent.

Here is a simple tool to help you move through your triggers. This tool is so simple that you may discount it, but stay with me and keep reading. I promise it will help. The tool is deep breathing.

In order to fully embrace the grief cycle, we need to learn more about breathing. The power of a deep intentional breath is highly underrated and far too many of us never tap into it. In my humble opinion, meditative breathing should be taught in kindergarten, right alongside reading and writing.

It wasn't until I was 48 that I experienced my first guided meditation. I was on the Hawaiian island of Kauai with my mom and sisters. After a long day of canoeing, hiking, and exploring, my youngest sister Megan invited everyone on a sunrise hike the following morning. I was the only one up for it, so despite my sore knees and the muddy climb, we hiked to the top of Okolehao Trail just in time for the sunrise. Meg insisted we sit side by side, cross legged on the ground. She played a guided meditation and took my hand. Listening to the woman's calm and soothing voice guided us to another place in our heads, and I began to relax. I welcomed the warmth of the sun on my face and focused on my breathing. I went to a place in my mind where I could be with my father, who had passed away the year before. There we were, me and my Papa Tom, together, even though he hadn't physically been with me in almost a year. It was nothing I'd ever experienced before, and it was everything I needed. It was the beginning of a new life for me, which included a lot more breathing.

A few weeks after losing my son, I was grocery shopping and having a pretty good day when suddenly I heard a baby crying in the next aisle. The cries immediately took me back to the hospital room where I delivered Baby Kevin. His cry was different from my other seven children's newborn cries. His didn't come as naturally, and took a lot more effort, like he was struggling to breathe.

That baby's cry in the grocery store sounded so similar to my son's, and I didn't see it coming. I stopped in my tracks, just standing there listening as my eyes filled with tears. I thought of my baby and how I missed him terribly. Rather than resist the emotions, I felt them. As I allowed the sadness to wash over me and urged myself to breathe, my heart rate slowly returned to normal, and I was able to finish my shopping.

A deep, intentional breath is a healthy and healing way to move through your triggers. I have since learned the power of a deep, intentional breath. Over time, I've adopted the practice of immediately taking deep breaths anytime an uncomfortable emotion hits, not just when grief surfaces.

Two things I love about breathing: first, you can do it anytime, anywhere, and no one notices. Second, it's one of the healthiest and fastest ways to bring you into the present moment, where we do our most effective healing.

In my grief coaching practice I teach the power of "flipping the switch." You can flip the switch on painful emotion when you allow the feeling to move through you, while taking three deep breaths (or as many as you need).

Right now, wherever you're reading this, I invite you to pause with me and practice flipping the switch. I'll guide you through it. Close your eyes if you're able to, and take a deep breath in through your nose, repeating these words in your head or out loud: "I'm okay." Breathe out through your nose. As you take a second breath in, repeat the words, "You're okay _____ (insert your own name)," then slowly breathe out. With the last breath repeat, "Everything is okay." You may disagree with that one; if so, try saying, "Everything is *going to be* okay." You can picture your Savior saying these reassuring words to you if you like. Repeat the sequence as many times as you need and as often as you desire. Please hear me when I tell you it's perfectly okay to sit in your sadness, despair, frustration, anger, or whatever emotion comes up for you, as long as you let it move through you. It turns into a problem when you resist the emotion or sit in it, without allowing it to move through you, causing the emotion to become trapped inside you. When that happens, you become the sadness, anger, frustration, sorrow, etc.

Accepting your feelings as they are can be helpful in allowing them in. It's okay to feel mad, sad, forgotten, disappointed, betrayed, overlooked, etc. When emotions trigger uncomfortable feelings, repeat these words out loud, or in your mind, "It's okay that I feel _____ . It's okay that I feel _____." That gives your mind and body permission to relax and sit in your current reality.

Dr. Jill Bolte Taylor's 90-Second rule[3] says that when you have a reaction to something in your environment (aka, you're triggered), a 90-second chemical process happens. If you just allow yourself to feel the feeling coming from the emotion, and breathe your way through it, it will usually pass within about 90 seconds. However, if you resist the feeling, it gets stuck inside you, making it far more difficult to process, especially if it gets lost in a sea of other trapped emotions.

Sad to say, I didn't learn the power of breath until my late 40's. To be honest, I resisted it at first. I'm a recovering control

---

3. https://www.psychologytoday.com/ca/blog/the-right-mindset/202004/the-90-second-rule-builds-self-control

enthusiast and I've lived far too much of my life in fight or flight mode—making stillness and intentional breathing difficult to access. But as I've worked at it, I have come to see the power in taking the time to intentionally quiet my thoughts through breathing.

Today I embrace meditation and mindfulness. I love it so much that it has become a daily part of my morning devotions. I use this tool regularly to manage my emotions throughout the day, and it often puts me to sleep at night. I love the words of C.S. Lewis: "Long ago in the ancient world God breathed the breath of life into clay and it became a man. Then at each of our conversions the Spirit of God breathed into each of us and we were born again unto a living hope."[4] C. S. Lewis used the imagery of divine breath to symbolize the life-giving power of the Holy Spirit in redemption and renewal. The breath of life can give us access to the power of the Holy Spirit to help us live life in the present, and work through our painful triggers until they fade into quiet memories.

When a trigger comes, whether at church, the grocery store, at work, or just trying to get through your day, flip the switch and breathe your way through it. *I'm okay. You're okay. Every-*

---

4. https://dfisher2014dotcom.wordpress.com/2015/01/22/
   the-breath-of-life/

thing's okay. Or *everything is going to be okay.* And it's perfectly fine to sit in and feel through whatever emotion you need to feel.

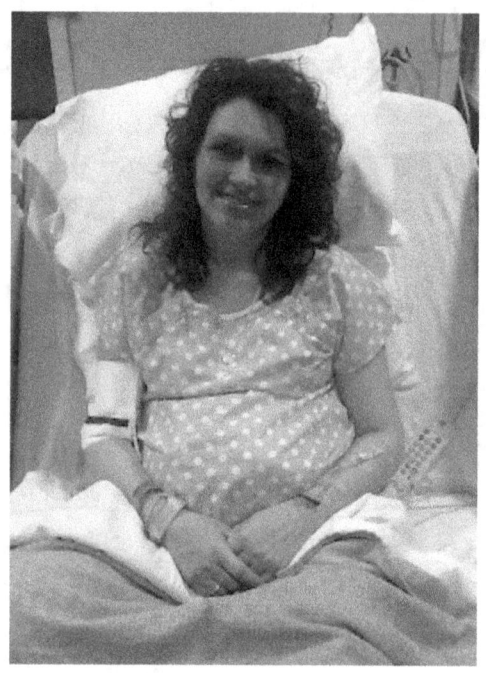

Questions to ponder

1. When was the last time you experienced a trigger? Was it a sweet reminder, painful, or bittersweet? How did you react to it?

2. When was the last time you intentionally took a deep breath?

3. Are there emotions and feelings you've been resisting that you need to accept and allow yourself to feel?

Invitation

Practice flipping the switch by taking three deep breaths (or as many as you'd like) to help you move through the feeling. Tell yourself, "I'm okay," "You're okay _____ (insert your name), "Everything is okay," or "Everything is going to be okay."

Try Dr. Bolte's 90-second rule as you continuously breathe deeply, feeling the triggered emotion, for 90 seconds. Remember, it's okay to feel whatever you are feeling. You can repeat to yourself, "It's okay that I'm feeling _____". Use these tools when triggers come.

2

—·—

BELIEVE

"BE NOT AFRAID, ONLY BELIEVE." MARK 5:36

On New Year's Day, my husband and I breathed a sigh of relief as we returned home. We had been driving through the night following a week in Arizona visiting my brother's family. I was 19 weeks pregnant and exhausted from sitting in the suburban so long and being awake most of the night. As I approached our porch I noticed a tiny gift bag near the door, a birthday present to me from my neighbor. Inside was a little beaded white and blue bracelet with the word "Believe" spelled out in tiny blocks. I'd turned 40 on Christmas Eve and wondered how long the gift had been sitting on my porch.

Later that day I received a phone call from Fetal Fotos. The ultrasound on my 40th birthday the week before showed a problem with the images of our son's face and recommended I schedule an appointment with my midwife for another ultrasound as soon as possible. I hung up the phone, completely confused. *A problem with his face?,* I wondered. What did that even mean? I shared the news with my husband and he assured me everything was probably fine and there was no reason to worry until we were able to see my midwife. I already had an appointment with her in a few days, so we would know soon enough.

Even with my husband's assurances, I felt very unsettled. I tried to distract myself by unpacking and doing laundry. We had a family night planned for later in the evening, so I went to my scriptures to find a verse to go along with the gospel message we would be discussing. When I opened the Bible, I looked down and one verse practically jumped off the page at me. "Be not afraid, only believe" (Mark 5:36). I had been trying my best to avoid fearful thoughts all day. And then that word *believe* surfaced again—just like on the bracelet. I knew it wasn't a coincidence.

I felt the Lord speaking to me, letting me know that while I had no idea what was going on with our baby, He did. It was as if He were saying, "Just have faith Becky, trust me, everything will be okay". What else could I do? I knew in that moment I had a choice, I could live in fear, worry and anxiety, or, I could simply trust Jesus. So I went with the latter and chose to trust Him. Just to be clear, I am a human, and doubts and anxiety did try to creep in, but never for long. My Savior continually comforted and reminded me, in the moments I needed Him most, *Be not afraid, only believe.*

The same message surfaced repeatedly throughout my pregnancy, and continues to show up now and again, at just the right times. *Be not afraid, only believe.*

Just a few years ago our son Dakota had been involved in a car accident. Thankfully he came away unharmed, but our car was totalled. At the time, I was also deeply troubled over a situation with one of my daughters. I decided to take my concerns to my dad. Before he passed away, I could just pick up the phone and call him, or drive the eight minutes to his house when I wanted to talk to him. Now that he's gone, when I want to speak to him, I usually do it while I'm driving. I recorded my conversation in the car with him that day in my journal:

> *On my drive home I decided to talk to my dad, update him on things, and tell him about Dakota's car accident. I thanked him if he'd had a hand in keeping him safe. Then I told him how I had been praying for my daughter and all the challenges she'd been facing. As I was explaining all of this to my father, I glanced up and saw the license plate on the car in front of me with the letters "BELEEVE". Are you kidding me? With or without the creative spelling, I got the message. I rarely get that message any more, but in that moment I was reminded that God knows exactly what He is doing with our girl. There is absolutely a plan in place. And*

everything will be just fine. I felt that I should call my daughter and share my experience. We were both emotional as I assured her that things were going to be okay. I think the Lord, Papa Tom, and Baby Kevin all wanted her to know of their love for her and that everything would work out. God is good. I wonder if sometimes we are so wrapped up in the stress of things that He needs to send answers through someone else.

I invite you, wherever you stand on your grief journey, to turn everything over to Jesus Christ and choose to trust Him. Believe He is aware of you, Believe He knows in a very intimate way, exactly what you are going through. Have faith and trust in the Lord and His assurances. In the Garden of Gethsemane, He not only suffered personally for your sins, but also for every pain, disappointment, and sorrow you would experience throughout your life. Believe that He will help you get through your darkest and most difficult hours of grief because He understands exactly what you're going through. He gets it, He gets you, and He can help in ways no one else can. I know this because He did it for me and I could not have survived my grief journey without Him.

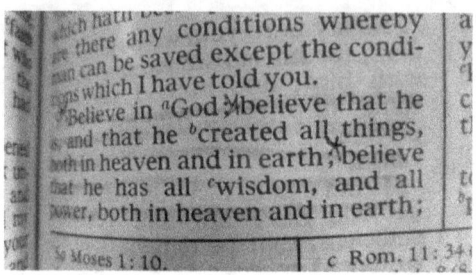

Questions to Ponder

1. On a scale of 0 (never) to 10 (always), how often have you turned to Christ for help on your grief journey?

2. On a scale of 0 to 10, how much do you trust your Savior to help you?

3. Is there an area of your grief that is particularly heavy right now? How would it feel if you allowed Christ to share that burden with you? What gets in your way?

Invitation

Choose one area of your life to turn over to Christ. Pray for help to let that thing go, and then believe He can and will help you.

3

TAKE COURAGE

"WAIT ON THE LORD: BE OF GOOD COURAGE, AND HE SHALL STRENGTHEN THINE HEART: WAIT, I SAY, ON THE LORD." PSALM 27:14

Let me begin by praising you for having the courage to buy this book. It takes courage to show up every day after you lose someone whose life was so intertwined with yours. It takes courage to navigate the pain and heartache that accompanies grief. It takes courage to create a new life after losing a child, spouse, parent, sibling or friend. The fact that you bought a book about grief, while you're already eating, sleeping, and breathing grief, tells me you may be ready to feel better, to have some measure of control over your grief journey, and you definitely want to feel more joy than you're currently experiencing. Am I right? You can live a blessed life, even without that person you loved so much. Seriously, you are amazing! Stick with me, keep turning these pages, and together we'll learn how to experience more joy in the present.

About a year ago I was anxious and hesitant to take some steps in my coaching business. Fear was holding me back. I went to the scriptures for direction from God about courage. When Jesus says, "Ask and ye shall receive," He's serious, and His answers are better than any google search I've ever found. The Savior taught me that courage isn't something you're born with, or something you have to give all your energy to muster up. It's not even something you have to wait to be gifted with. It's just there for the taking—you and I can "take courage" if we choose to take it. The scriptures repeatedly talk of *being of good courage*, or in other words—trusting in the Lord as your true source of strength.

So how do you do that? How do you take courage and be of good courage when you are drowning in grief? It's not easy. It requires intentionally working through your grief. It means not avoiding, going around, or skipping over, but rather, walking right into your grief. It means feeling all your feelings rather than resisting or avoiding them. And it means being open, and receiving the Lord's plan for you. It's believing that despite how hard your life is right now, an all-knowing and loving Father in Heaven is working all things for your good.

Having said that, I've noticed patterns that lead to the choice to take courage, my very favorites being the patterns of prayer and assurances. As we pray in faith to God and receive assurances from the Lord through His Spirit, we are able to see the reminders He sends to let us know He is aware of us, He loves us, He can help us, and that everything is going to be alright—eventually.

In the days following the news that the baby boy I'd been carrying for four and a half months was not going to live, doctors warned me he could pass away at any time. That caused me to be anxious over being alone or even leaving the house, for fear that I might miscarry. And then one day, in a quiet moment, I was filled with peace as the words entered my mind, "This pregnancy will be much like all your others and you'll deliver this baby full term." It was an assurance I couldn't deny. In that moment, I took courage. It took time, but I stopped worrying and began intentionally living my life every day. I took courage as I focused on the needs of my husband and seven other children. I took courage by booking a vacation to Boston with my sisters. And at five and a half months pregnant, Baby Kevin and I walked miles and miles together as we toured the beautiful city of Boston. I took courage every morning as I got up a few minutes before the family to talk to God and read scripture to help center myself and begin my day with peace. I filled my thoughts with good courage and trusted the Lord as my true source of strength. I relied on His strength from moment to moment as waves of anticipatory grief would come without warning. I took courage as I waited on the Lord to show me His will for my son and how to grieve my loss.

Helaman, an ancient prophet and military leader in The Book of Mormon: Another Testament of Jesus Christ,[1] shares the experience of his Nephite army. They had waited months for the government to send more strength and provisions to keep them from being destroyed by the much bigger and stronger Lamanite army. Conditions had become so terrible they feared they would soon die from starvation. The Nephites eventually received some food, but no other support. Helaman and his army were filled with anticipatory grief and fear.

So what did they do? In Alma 58:10-12 we learn, "Therefore we did pour out our souls in prayer to God, that he would strengthen us and deliver us out of the hands of our enemies, yea, and also give us strength that we might retain our cities, and our lands, and our possessions, for the support of our people." The result of that pleading prayer was, "The Lord our God did visit us with assurances that he would deliver us; yea, insomuch that he did speak peace to our souls [and couldn't we all use more of that], and did grant unto us great faith, and did cause us that we should hope for our deliverance in him." Because of those assurances, Helaman proclaims, "We did take courage

---

1. Just as the Bible is a record of God's dealings with His children in the Holy Land, the Book of Mormon is a record of God's dealings with His children in the Americas following His resurrection.

with our small force which we had received, and were fixed with a determination to conquer our enemies, and to maintain our lands, and our possessions, and our wives, and our children, and the cause of our liberty."

The result was Helaman and his small army, with the help of the Lord and His power, won the battle, and in the process, recovered all of their cities from the Lamanites. And then Helaman gives God the glory in verses 33 and 37, "But behold, we trust in our God who has given us victory over those lands, insomuch that we have obtained those cities and those lands, which were our own." He goes on to proclaim, "We trust God will deliver us, notwithstanding the weakness of our armies, yea, and deliver us out of the hands of our enemies."

You too can pour out your soul in prayer to God for strength and trust that the Lord will help you through your grief. He can and will deliver you through the pain and loss you're currently experiencing as you take courage, be of good courage, and have the faith to trust your Savior as you turn to Him for help.

I can assure you, the Lord is in the details of your loss. Every moment of every day and especially when you're feeling alone in your grief, He's right there beside you. I invite you to continue to take courage on your grief journey by praying to the Lord humbly and often. Seek those assurances He so freely gives—and when you find them (which you will), take hold of them and don't let go. Put your assurances on paper so you can go back and remember the Lord's hand in your grief when you're having a particularly hard day. Have the courage to keep reading this book, even when you don't feel like reading. You can put it aside when you need a break, then pick it up again so your Savior can help you create a new life filled with blessings of hope, peace and joy—and not just a fleeting joy, but a steady abiding joy you won't ever want to live without.

And please believe me when I tell you, it's never too late to embrace the grief cycle. I'm going to say it again, because I really want you to hear me: it's never too late to embrace the grief cycle. Even if you've been avoiding the pain of your grief for years, or maybe you're stuck in anger, depression or denial. Wherever you are on your grief journey, I promise you, if you will take courage by taking even the smallest of steps into the grief cycle, it will be worth the effort.

Questions to Ponder

1. Is there an area of grief you feel stuck in? Maybe denial, anger, or depression?

2. How often do you have the courage to pray to your Father in Heaven for help?

3. What assurances has the Lord given you on your grief journey? If you struggle to remember, ask Him to remind you of past assurances and watch for more to come.

Invitation

Pray and ask the Lord to help you see the assurances He is sending you, and then record them so you won't forget. Be sure to thank Him for the assurances He gives you.

4

—·—

THE GRIEF CYCLE

"FOR I WILL TURN THEIR MOURNING INTO JOY, AND WILL COMFORT THEM, AND MAKE THEM REJOICE FROM THEIR SORROW." JEREMIAH 31:13

"Maybe it's time to get over it and just move on," said a neighbor to my friend who lost her husband. It had been two years since her husband's death and her grief was still incredibly heavy. Do those words make your blood boil like they do mine? However well-meaning this neighbor was trying to be, it was a terrible thing for my friend to hear.

It doesn't matter if your loss occurred last week, last month, or several years ago; you don't just "get over it." People who say those things don't understand grief. But I do believe you can "get through it". You will be okay. You will move forward. And you will find joys you didn't realize were possible as you learn to embrace the grief cycle.

Let's define what the grief cycle is and what it is not. The grief cycle is not the same as the five stages of grief,[1] which include denial, anger, bargaining, depression, and acceptance. However, the grief cycle is a resource to help you move through the five stages of grief, especially if you find yourself lost in denial, stuck in anger, obsessed with bargaining, or buried in depression.

The grief cycle has four parts:

1. Mourn

2. Lament

3. Be Grateful

4. Celebrate

Each of these four parts work together, supporting each other, so you can access joy—no matter how difficult and heavy your current circumstance may be. Step into the grief cycle wherever and whenever you want, and in the smallest and sim-

---

1. For a brief discussion of the five stages of grief, see https://www.cruse.org.uk/understanding-grief/effects-of-grief/five-stages-of-grief/, which summarizes the classic work of Elizabeth Kubler Ross in her book On Death and Dying in 1969.

plest of ways. There isn't one area of the cycle that is better than another, and there's no order to it. The more areas of your life you choose to live in the grief cycle, the more help, peace, healing, and joy you'll find as you navigate through your season of grief.

There is no right or wrong way to mourn, lament, practice gratitude, and celebrate. Do what feels most comfortable, and keep it simple at first. Floors and ceilings is a great way to approach any new task or habit you'd like to create. A floor is a simplified version of any habit. A floor can take one minute or less to do. A floor should be *almost* effortless, so you can do it practically anytime, anywhere. You may be tempted to discount a floor because you believe it's too easy, or not even worth doing, but I promise you, even the smallest of efforts pay dividends immediately or eventually. In contrast, a ceiling is the ideal of what your task or habit would look like.

For instance, let's say you want to start journaling each day. Your floor might be writing one word to describe your day, while your ceiling might be a paragraph, describing in great detail, what you felt and experienced throughout your day. Whether you journal a word or a paragraph, praise yourself for the effort, with zero guilt or judgment. You can always raise your floor. You can add a sentence to the word. You can switch from a sentence to a short audio recording instead. You can also lower your ceiling, by simplifying: skipping the paragraph and writing only a sentence. Remember, when your grief is feeling heavy, the goal is always a floor—anything more than that is a bonus.

Floors and ceilings can be applied to all sorts of things you want or need to be doing. I remember heading into summertime a few weeks after our son's passing. Summers with a house full of children had always been busy for me. There were years we spent a day or two each week at the water park where I'd be chasing my little ones around the kiddie pool, or riding the slides with the older ones. As a mother, I was really good at hitting ceilings for summer time. But this particular summer I was recovering from childbirth, I was tired, and I was grieving every day. I didn't have it in me to hit the ceiling and take everyone to the waterpark for the day, frequently throughout the summer. But I could do a floor, so instead I took them to the city pool for an hour or two. The first time we went, I didn't even bother to get in the water. I literally just sat on the floor by the pool, watched the kids play, wrote in my journal, and allowed myself to grieve surrounded by a bunch of parents with their noisy kids splashing around, having fun. I both mourned and lamented as I journaled about how unsettled I was feeling. Here are a few things I wrote:

> *I brought the kids to the city pool. They are swimming, I am sitting. I am so tired. This whole baby situation has done me in. I just need a break from financial and business stresses. I can't handle go-*

ing into the office and having to play catch-up at home. I know I need to change my attitude, but I'm emotionally spent. It doesn't help that I'm sitting at the pool looking all chubby in my swimsuit, still toting extra pounds of baby weight. I do feel like there is something positive just around the corner. I hope there is.

Although nothing changed that particular day. Eventually, we turned the corner and things got better. The result of me doing the floor version of a swim day were happy kids and some time well-spent grieving, getting it on paper and out of my head.

I took the kids to the city pool a few more times that summer. I guess I could have felt bad that I didn't get season passes to the water park. I could have been disappointed in myself for not going to the pool more often and packing the big picnic lunches the kids loved. I could have beat myself up over not getting in the water to play with them. But I didn't. I allowed myself time to grieve, gave myself permission to do less, dropped "the should's," and had the courage to do only a floor. And you know what? My kids had a great summer, and mine was pretty good too.

I encourage you to create floors as you begin to mourn, lament, practice gratitude, and celebrate as you move through your grief. A floor is always the perfect place to start.

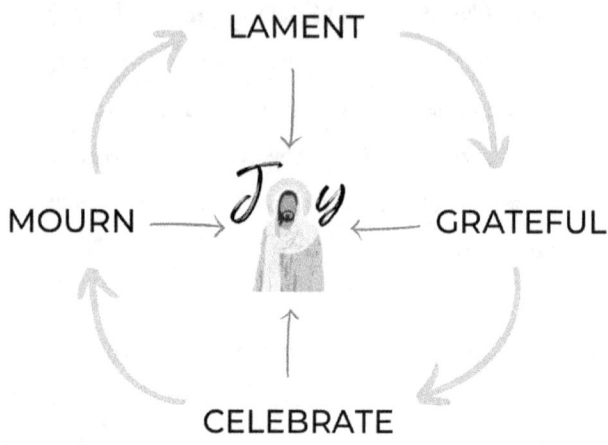

Questions to Ponder

1. Have you included mourning, lamenting, gratitude and celebration in your grieving?

2. Which of these four areas resonate most with you?

3. What is a floor you already have in place for one of your habits? Is it helping you through your grief?

Invitation

Is there a habit you've been wanting to create, or one you'd like to get back to, that might help you feel better as you continue to grieve? Create a floor for that habit (remember, floors only take a minute or less), and try doing it once a day.

5

MEANT FOR JOY

"BUT THE FRUIT OF THE SPIRIT IS LOVE, JOY, PEACE…"   GALATIANS 5:22

Miserable-joy is the term my friend Cathi uses for experiencing grief and joy simultaneously. Wow, did I feel miserable-joy throughout the second half of my pregnancy. I guess you could say the first 20 weeks were filled with more of an ignorant-joy. Aside from morning, noon, and night sickness; my days were pure bliss as I anticipated the birth of our eighth child, who I assumed would be a healthy baby boy. I loved the idea of having our entire family together under one roof for the few months before our oldest son Jackson went away to college. At 10 weeks pregnant I wrote in my journal:

> *Tomorrow we have our first ultrasound. I'm excited about that! I am feeling so grateful for all that is happening at this stage of my life. The kids*

bring me so much joy and it's fun to watch them
experience life in all their different stages.

Those first weeks of my pregnancy were filled with so much happiness and anticipation. The weeks following, while filled with disappointment and sorrow, drew me closer to my Savior and He helped me find joy and happiness too. I look back on both types of joy – miserable-joy and ignorant-joy – with gratitude, love, and reverence as I learned the beauty of living a life of joy in both extremes.

I believe, at the heart of every human, is the desire to be happy and have true and lasting joy. However, happiness is different from joy. Happiness is consumed, while joy is created. Happiness can come and go and has limits because it is dependent upon external factors. Joy, on the other hand, is more than a fleeting emotion or feeling. Joy runs deep and embraces the heart and soul. Joy is bigger than happiness and has zero limits because joy can exist in any circumstance. Joy is both a gift and a fruit of the Spirit. Joy must be received, planted, and nurtured intentionally in order for the fruit to grow.

As you accept the gift of joy and partake of its fruits, you will be filled with peace and comfort—the two things longed for most in the midst of grief. And the thing I love most about joy—the greater your challenge, hardship, or loss, the greater your capacity becomes for experiencing joy.

In the introduction of this book I shared my belief that our Father in Heaven created us to have joy in any circumstance: in the good times, in the hard times, and especially through the depths of grief and despair. In The Book of Mormon, the Lord's prophet Lehi proclaims, "Adam fell that men might be; and men are, that they might have joy" (1 Nephi 2:25). In other words, you and I, and all mankind were born into this world to experience joy, and not just around holidays, weddings, birthdays, and vacations, or when everything is going right. Joy is the very reason for our existence. We came wired for it. Joy is available 24 hours a day, seven days a week. Joy is the reason our Lord and Savior endured the suffering, "Who for the joy that was set before him endured the cross, despising the shame, and is set down at the right hand of the throne of God" (Hebrews 12:2). Because of Jesus Christ and His sacrifice for us, there is no shortage of joy, and no parameters around when and where we can receive it. And yet, so many of God's children lack the blessings of joy in their lives, with the false belief that joy is based on circumstance, rather than a continuous gift the Lord gives to all who are willing to receive it.

As I read through my old journals I see joy as a common theme throughout the days and months surrounding the loss of my son and later, my father. Joy was a constant companion to my grief. The two ran parallel to each other and the joy is what made the grief manageable. Joy became a lifeline—helping me survive the really hard days.

While on vacation with my sisters in Boston, I had a couple of really emotional days. I was 24 weeks pregnant, knowing the baby wouldn't survive long. I'd been trying to manage my thoughts and feelings of sadness and confusion over what lay ahead, and I was incredibly tired mentally and physically. My sisters and I did most of our traveling on foot and by subway. We rarely had to wait for a train, but this particular night, we waited. A few steps from us a man with a mandolin began playing the hymn "Be Still My Soul." As I sat in the calmness of the music, I felt the love of the Lord and the enabling power of His Atonement giving me strength. Peace filled my heart and joy washed over me.

Weeks later, before leaving for a checkup and ultrasound with my doctor, I tucked a small book into my purse, a gift from a friend.[1] The book is based on the scripture, "love life, and see good days" (1 Peter 3:10). The author invited me to trust the Savior's promises, shift my perspective a bit, and let go of the things that don't matter so much. It all sounded nice, but I wondered if it were possible to see any good on doctor appointment days. The excitement I used to feel at the prospect of seeing and hearing my baby's heartbeat, had been replaced

---

1. Love Life and See Good Days by Emily Belle Freeman https://www.amazon.com/Love-Life-See-Good-Days/dp/1629723363

with hope and dread. We were always hoping that we'd see some part of his body had healed (we almost never did), and dreading what new problems might be found (there were usually a few).

I sat in the waiting room, opened the book, and as I began to read I felt Jesus waiting there with me. He taught me that on hard days, I could pray in faith to see the good and He would help me find it. I took Jesus and that book to the rest of my doctor appointments. With His help I began finding more good in my hard days, and feeling the joy that accompanied it.

There's no shortage of joy our loving God has to offer us. There is good to see and joy to feel, even in the hardest of days. You have the ability, with the help of Jesus Christ, to create and become joy. As you live in The Grief Cycle by intentionally taking time to mourn, lament, be grateful, and celebrate, you will find joy in the midst of your grief.

Questions to Ponder

1. Have there been times in your life where you experienced miserable-joy? What was that like?

2. How about ignorant-joy?

3. Have you invented any other hyphenated joys?

4. What brings you joy, even just a little bit?

Invitations

I invite you to simply believe there is joy to be found as you live the grief cycle. Pray to see the good in your days and feel the joy it can produce. Believe the Savior will help you to see the good you might be missing so you can feel the joy and peace He can give you.

6

— • —

FINDING JOY IN THE MOURNING

"BLESSED ARE ALL THEY THAT MOURN FOR THEY SHALL BE COMFORTED." 3 NEPHI 12:4

G oing for further tests, my husband and I walked hand in hand through the door of the medical imaging center in St Mark's Hospital. Fear and worry kept trying to push their way into my head and it was all I could do to battle them with all the hopeful thoughts I could muster. *Everything will be okay. Things aren't as bad as they seem. Ultrasounds can be wrong.*

Before long my name was called and we were led to an exam room. The ultrasound technician did a thorough scan of our son's body and her findings weren't good. She not only confirmed the problem in our baby's heart and brain, but she also saw a bilateral cleft palate. When she finished, a doctor came in and reviewed the technician's notes and performed another careful scan. Two areas of the brain were much bigger than normal. The bilateral calcification of his heart, along with the cleft palate, all pointed toward Trisomy 13 or Trisomy 18.

I was familiar with Trisomy 21, also known as Down Syndrome. Down Syndrome babies have an average life expectancy of 60 years. Although they experience learning and developmental delays and possibly health problems, many children born with Down syndrome can grow up to be independent. On the other hand, babies born with Trisomy 13 or 18 generally do not survive their first year of life, and those who do are severely disabled.

I went into this appointment knowing there were problems, but this news was so much worse than anything I could have anticipated. Given all our son had working against him, it was a miracle he'd survived so far. I was crushed. Completely devastated. Escaping to the bathroom, I shut the door and totally lost it. I cried for as long as I thought I could get away with before Kevin came in after me. In that hospital bathroom, I mourned the loss of my son; it was the first of many, many times I would mourn him throughout my anticipatory grief and the grief following his passing.

I've learned quite a bit about mourning since then. I've come to realize that mourning and grieving are not the same thing. Grieving is internal; mourning is external. To grieve is what we think and feel on the inside after a loss as we seek to give it meaning. It's the feelings of fear, loneliness, panic, pain, yearning, anxiety, emptiness etc. In contrast, mourning is to outwardly express our grief. It's talking it out, crying it out, writing it out, perhaps using art, music and movement as a means of expressing our grief. Those tears I shed in the bathroom after receiving the devastating news about our son were tears of mourning. It was a relief to get them out. I walked out of the bathroom and onto a long, grief-filled road ahead, but after releasing that first batch of tears, I felt a tiny bit better. Every time I mourned going forward, it was the mourning – the outward expression of my grieving – which kept the grief moving through me.

There are many ways to outwardly mourn, like journaling your thoughts and feelings or writing a letter to your loved one. Talk about how you feel. Find a friend or two who can listen with love, and without judgment. Expressing my grief through listening to music is one of the most healing ways for me to mourn. I recorded in my journal an experience I had one particular morning while worshipping:

> *I heard the Polynesians in the back of the chapel singing in their language, but I knew the English words to the familiar hymn: "May my heart, be turned to pray, pray in secret, day by day, that this boon, to mortals giv'n, may unite my soul with*

heaven...".[1] The Spirit of the Lord was so strong I could hardly hold back the tears. At that moment I didn't care how long I had to sit, I didn't want that music or feeling to end.

The song reminded me that it was my private prayers to the Lord that had so often comforted and supported me in my grief. I was filled with gratitude to my God for his willingness to listen and be with me whenever I needed him.

Jesus taught the order to grief while teaching the Sermon on the Mount in Matthew 5. He proclaimed the promise, "Blessed are they that mourn: for they shall be comforted" (verse 4). The ancient prophet Alma taught the baptismal covenant: we are to be "willing to bear one another's burdens, that they may be light, mourn with those that mourn and comfort those that stand in need of comfort" (Mosiah 18:8-9). Notice both the Savior and His prophet Alma mention mourn first, and then comfort.

Often, when we are trying to help bear one another's burdens, we skip the mourning and go right to the comforting. And yet, the current reality for someone who has just lost their loved one is that they may not be ready to be comforted. They are in

---

1. https://www.churchofjesuschrist.org/music/library/hymns/secret-prayer?lang=eng

a great deal of pain, and they're left with a pretty big void in their life and hole in their heart. They have every right to sit in their current reality and take time to mourn for as long as they need or want to. If we are willing, at times we can sit and mourn with them. On the other hand, comforting focuses on a future reality. When they are ready to be comforted, we can help with that too.

If you are reading this book, your current reality may be that you've lost someone you love very much. You know what it's like to feel the void of your loss and the pains of a broken heart. Sitting in your current reality and giving yourself permission and time to mourn your loss is essential to healing and eventually feeling ready to receive comfort.

I watched my mother grieve after my dad's passing. At first she felt a measure of relief because all the pain he had endured from prostate cancer and its treatment had finally ended. She found peace and comfort knowing he was in a better place, and that his suffering was over. She had faith, believing she would see him again, trusting that their separation was temporary. While my mom did mourn outwardly at times, she relied mostly on the comforting. She also relied on distraction. Her home needed a lot of repairs which became her full time job. Just as she'd get one thing fixed, something else would surface. I think her basement flooded three times the first year after my dad passed away in December 2018.

Fast-forward to March 2020. The pandemic shut down the world, her city experienced a significant earthquake, and she was housebound, with nothing left to repair. Suddenly Mom had quite a bit of time on her hands. You know what she finally did? She mourned. She mourned the passing of her sweetheart fifteen months earlier. She mourned and mourned and mourned some more. She couldn't avoid it—not that she ever intentionally tried to—but the distractions got the best of her. But she couldn't fully heal without mourning. Her mind and body needed more than comfort; she needed to mourn.

The experience recorded in John 11 of Mary and Martha mourning their brother Lazarus is a beautiful example. One of these two sisters was ready for comfort and the other needed to mourn. Before Lazarus's death the sisters sent a message to Jesus: "He whom thou lovest is sick" (verse 6). Jesus received the message, but deliberately delayed for two days (verse 6). By the time He arrived, Lazarus had "lain in the grave four days already" (verse 17). Lazarus's sisters were grieving and many came to offer comfort (verse 19).

When Jesus was coming, Martha went out to meet Him to be comforted, while Mary stayed home to grieve. When Martha saw Jesus she lamented, "Lord, if thou hadst been here, my brother had not died. But I know, that even now, whatsoever thou wilt ask of God, God will give it thee" (verses 21-22). Martha mourned the loss of her brother, and was then ready for Jesus's comforting words, "Thy brother shall rise again" (verse

23). Eventually Martha sent a message to Mary, "The Master is come, and calleth for thee" (verse 28). Mary immediately hurried to Jesus and fell at His feet. She too lamented, "Lord, if thou hadst been here my brother had not died" (verse 32). But Jesus gave her no comforting words. Instead, she wept, and when Jesus saw it, He also wept (verse 35). In short, Jesus honored Martha by offering the comfort she needed, and Jesus honored Mary by allowing her space to mourn, taking the time to mourn with her.

Are you like Martha, in need of encouragement and comfort? Or are you like Mary, and just need to mourn through your tears? Mourning and comforting aren't a one-and-done experience. They are both needful. You can draw on the blessings both offer, as often as you need them.

Opportunities to mourn often come without warning, but they can also be created intentionally. One of the things I found to be most helpful was taking time to mourn daily. Including mourning in my nightly and morning routines created an opportunity for me to center myself, heal, and regularly give my emotions an outlet. This allowed my mind and body to be able to do the things I needed and wanted to for my family and myself without being immobilized by trapped internal grief.

When God created the earth, He set the pattern for how to begin each day: when He proclaimed, "And the evening and the morning were the first day" (Genesis 1:5). Notice that instead of thinking of a day as starting in the morning, God's day began in the evening. He repeated this pattern with the creation of each day, suggesting that our days begin the night before. We can be intentional in how we spend our time right before bed and when we first get up, setting the stage for the rest of our day. I remember talking to God and shedding many tears right before I fell asleep at night. Then each morning I got up a few minutes before the family so I could have quiet time to journal my thoughts and feelings, pray for help to get through my day, and read a few verses of scripture to remind me of the power and goodness of God. I found so much peace and joy as I intentionally took time to mourn in my evenings and my mornings. Perhaps other times of the day work better for you, but these holy times have worked for me.

These spaces of time before bed and first thing in the morning became sacred hours of my day. Crying it out, talking things out with God, and putting thoughts and feelings on paper, all help free up brain and heart space, so you'll have room for the variety of experiences waiting for you throughout the day. And yet it's easy to fall into the trap of numbing out right before bed by watching television or scrolling social media and the internet; then reaching for the phone when we first wake up to check an inbox, play a game, or check in with social media. This habit may keep us in the mind of the world as we go to bed, staying with us as we sleep, and is right there waiting for us when we wake up—giving us a dose of anxiousness which sends our body into fight or flight mode, where mourning and healing is more difficult. Like my mom postponing grieving by keeping constantly busy, our bedtime and morning routines can block out grief.

As you give yourself permission to mourn by outwardly expressing your grief, you make room for joy to enter into your heart and aid in your healing. Making time to intentionally mourn, even if it's only a few minutes before bed and after waking, will bless your days and give your brain more time to rest from so much input.

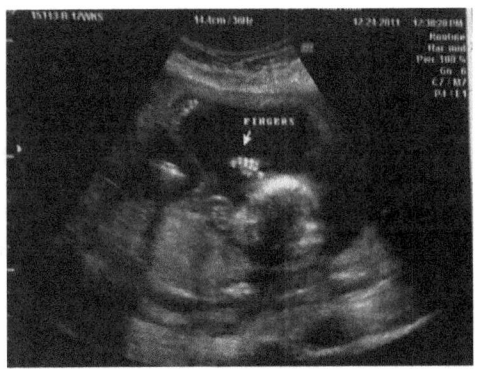

Questions to Ponder

1. Have you been mourning your loss (external), or mostly grieving (internal)?

2. Are you taking time to mourn each day, or have you focused on distractions like home projects or digital devices?

Invitation

I invite you to disconnect from the digital world and set aside a few minutes, before bed and when you first wake up, to intentionally mourn the loss of your loved one. Choose one simple way to outwardly express your grief each morning and night. Even after the grief begins to dissipate, disconnecting from the world in the morning and evenings is a habit I continue to practice. It helps me clear my head and connect with myself and the Lord.

7

—— • ——

FINDING JOY IN THE LAMENTING

"THAT YE SHALL WEEP AND LAMENT, BUT THE WORLD SHALL REJOICE: AND YE SHALL BE SORROWFUL, BUT YOUR SORROW SHALL BE TURNED INTO JOY."   JOHN 15:20

I had the privilege to help care for my father during his last months of life. Watching him suffer was one of the most difficult things I've ever gone through, and yet our time spent together was sacred. Anyone who has watched someone they love pass away from cancer knows it's a pretty terrible way to die. Before prostate cancer took him, Papa Tom had one of the biggest servant's hearts I've ever known. He always played ready. Ready to fix almost anything that needed fixing. Ready to listen. Ready to give praise and counsel. Ready to teach and testify.

And ready to give a priesthood[1] blessing to anyone who needed it. Dad was a true follower of Jesus Christ and shared Christ wherever he went. When he was in hospice, he even prayed over one of his nurses when he learned she was struggling financially and trying to find more work. Together, they held hands as he forgot his dying self and asked God to bless his nurse with more work so she could pay her bills. My dad couldn't eat by mouth, couldn't get around the house without assistance from one and sometimes two people, but he could pray for his nurse who needed help. As I watched him racked with pain day after day, I often wondered to myself, *Why does Dad, who has lived such a good life, have to experience so much suffering?* I didn't have any answers for that.

After my father passed, my mind continued to be troubled by that question. If I had understood the gift of lamenting back then, I probably would have lamented over many things surrounding his death, but instead, I held that one question in my heart. It sat there for months, unanswered, until one particularly hard day. I was overwhelmed with motherhood, stressed

---

1. In The Church of Jesus Christ of Latter-day Saints a priesthood blessing is given by a Melchizedek Priesthood holder, by the laying on of hands and by inspiration, to one who is sick or otherwise in need of special counsel, comfort, or healing.

that I might be pregnant at age 47 (false alarm), frustrated with some things going on with our business, and trying to figure out my new place as the bishop's wife. But most of all, I missed my dad. Had he been there, I would have gone to him for advice. He always knew just what to say. I always found comfort in his wisdom and perspective. And then there was that lingering question of why he had to go through so much suffering. I felt pretty brokenhearted that day, which may have been why my heart had room for the Lord to speak these reassuring words in my mind: "In time you will understand why your dad experienced so much suffering."

I waited in faith another eighteen months before the answer came. Sitting on an airplane headed home from visiting my son's family in Mesa, Arizona, I was immersed in a book when the understanding came. Tears flowed as the Spirit explained to my mind and heart, through feelings too sacred to share, why my father's last days were filled with so much suffering. The answer was simple, clear, and came from He who knows the end from the beginning. As I took my question to the Lord, in time, He answered, and blessed me with understanding. My heart was filled with joy as I received a glimpse of the love the Lord had for my father, and the love my father had for his Savior.

Since then, I have come to realize the important role lamenting plays in our grieving. So important, in fact, that an entire book in the Bible is dedicated to lamenting. It's even clearly named, The Lamentations of Jeremiah, or Lamentations for short. Thank you, Jeremiah, for calling out the miserable conditions of Jerusalem for what they were, instead of sugar-coating things, or ignoring them altogether. The Hebrew Bible mentions lamenting over sixty times, so it would seem that God is asking us to better understand what a lamentation is, how to do it, and why we should lament more often. In our rush to find comfort, we often skip over the gift of lamentation. So let's get specific on what it really means to lament.

You may be surprised to learn, as I was, that a lamentation is actually a prayer. A prayer specifically purposed to express your sorrow, heartache, and confusion to the Lord. A prayer for help in coming out of pain. And (I love this) a prayer designed to persuade God to act on the sufferer's behalf. Who couldn't use a little more of this type of prayer – a lamentation prayer? And not just when you're grieving a death; you can lament any time your reality is hard, anytime you feel anger, sadness, betrayal, or neglect. You can take all those things to the Lord, as often as you need to, and He'll help you work through them.

There are four steps to a lament prayer.

- First, turn to God in humility.

- Next, offer up your complaint.

- Then ask for his help and guidance.

- And finally, trust in His answers and timing.

I have always been really good at turning, asking, and trusting God. Complaining however, not so much. I believed to complain would be to murmur against God and I don't want to be disrespectful. But murmuring is not the same kind of complaining associated with a lament prayer. The two are actually very different.

In a lament prayer, you humbly *take your complaints to God*. Murmuring, on the other hand, is *complaining about God*. King David took his complaints to the Lord as he lamented, "My God, my God, why hast thou forsaken me? why art thou *so* far from helping me, and from the words of my roaring? O my God, I cry in the daytime, but thou hearest not; and in the night season, and am not silent" (Psalm 22:1-2). And in humility he adds, "But thou art holy, O thou that inhabitest the praises of Israel" (Psalm 22:3).

Turning to God, complaining to God, asking for His help, and trusting Him—all boils down to one word: surrender. When you humbly surrender your expectations, desires, emotions, and will to Him, true healing and sanctification can begin. When we yield our hearts to God, He can make our experience holy, replace beauty for ashes, turn tears of anguish into holy tears, and bring a level of joy into your grief you may not realize was possible. I think this scripture illustrates beautifully what happens when we humble ourselves and surrender our grief to

Him: "Be thou humble; and the Lord thy God shall lead thee by the hand, and give thee answer to thy prayers" (Doctrine & Covenants 112:10). And in the following verse the Lord gives this assurance, "I know thy heart, and have heard thy prayers...."

After learning the baby boy I was carrying probably wouldn't live, I humbly wrote a lament prayer to God in my journal:

> *I trust You completely. I trust in Your plan for me and my family. I trust I'll be able to raise this baby in the next life, but the human part of me is having a really hard time. My heart breaks for this little one and all of his challenges. If he were to live, I am scared for the challenges he and our family would be faced with. I'm sad for not being able to raise another son in this life—I've pictured him with our family for so long...I'm torn as to what to hope for from here. Part of me wants to have him with me as long as possible and deliver him alive so the kids have an opportunity to meet and hold their brother. Another part of me doesn't know if I could handle that and maybe it's best if he passes away as soon as possible. I don't know what to do other than continue to put my life and this baby's life in Your hands.*

Notice, the order of a lament prayer doesn't have to be perfect. I turned to God first, expressing my trust in Him, in humility I took my complaints to him, and then reaffirmed my trust in Him. Woven into my concerns was my asking Him for help to know what to hope for. After I wrote those words, I felt greater peace and clarity. I have learned that the Lord is just waiting patiently for us to turn to Him and ask for His help. If speaking your complaints to the Lord feels uncomfortable, try writing them instead.

As mentioned earlier, I was given the assurance that I would carry our son full term. Believing that, I began hoping for time with him after he was born. In our faith, babies are given a name and blessing shortly after birth. The thought that our baby may not live long enough to receive his name and blessing weighed heavily on my mind, so I took my concern to God. He answered my lament through a conversation with one of my church leaders, who explained how giving a name and blessing to a baby isn't an essential saving ordinance. I felt comforted knowing if our son passed away before he could be named and blessed, it would be alright. And I was grateful for the doctrine teaching that since little children are not accountable or capable of committing sinful acts, they don't need baptism. With every written and spoken lament prayer, I knew the Lord listened. Whether a direct answer, understanding, or someone else reaching out to me in one way or another, God always sent help. He always replied to my lament prayers in very personal ways. Our loving

Father in Heaven loves when we come to Him for help. I've learned He seldom gives us all the answers all at once. If that were the case, we would never learn or grow, or exercise faith. But He'll always give us enough to keep going, keep healing, and keep moving closer to the joy He has promised each of His children.

In scripture I've noticed where mourning is mentioned, lamenting is often nearby. The two go hand in hand. For example, after a tremendous battle with significant loss on both sides, "There was a great mourning and lamentation heard throughout all the land" (Alma 28:4). Another example is after a great battle between the Lamanites and the people of Limhi: "And now there was a great mourning and lamentation among the people of Limhi, the widow mourning for her husband, the son and the daughter mourning for their father, and the brothers for their brethren" (Mosiah 21:9).

Other words associated with lamenting in scripture are crying, weeping, wailing, and fasting. Lament prayer combined with a sincere and humble fast can activate heaven's help in miraculous ways. In the New Testament, the disciples of Jesus Christ couldn't cast out a devil (Mark 9:17-29). After the Savior came and cast the devil out, the disciples wanted to know why He was able to do it, when they couldn't. The Savior replied, "This kind can come forth by nothing, but by prayer and fasting" (verse 29). Or in other words, some things are so big to overcome that prayer alone isn't enough; sacrifice is also required.

In the months preceding my father's death, his pain became so severe he couldn't sleep.The cancer had invaded his bones—eating away at one side of his jaw. His mouth had filled with sores from a prior radiation treatment, which meant he wasn't able to eat. We begged and pleaded with the Lord to relieve his sufferings. We felt helpless. Not knowing what to do, some of the family decided to add a continuous fast to our lament prayers. Each of us chose a day of the week to fast, then the next person fasted the next day. For weeks we fasted for a miracle for our father. After two months of continuous fasting by someone in the family, Dad passed away. Our fast didn't heal him like we'd hoped, and oftentimes the pain remained, but we did see many joy-filled miracles throughout his last days, and we were given added strength to bear our part of his burden.

Through my own personal experience lamenting combined with fasting, I have become more humble, gained a deeper trust in the Lord, and my heart and mind have opened to seeing and receiving the joys that run parallel to my grief.

We humans actually come from a long line of lamenters. The first account I found was in the third book of Genesis where the Lord asks Adam, "Hast thou eaten of the tree, whereof I commanded thee that thou shouldest not eat?", to which Adam lamented, "The woman whom thou gavest to be with me, she gave me of the tree, and I did eat" (verse 12). Then Eve follows with her own lament in reply to the same question, "The serpent beguiled me, and I did eat" (verse 13). Notice how God responded: He took care of any potential problem his children might encounter on earth by giving them a Savior. God enabled our first earthly parents and all their posterity to survive being human in this fallen world and eventually return to Him. Not just survive, but thrive throughout our earthly experience, as we take upon us the name of Jesus Christ and draw upon the redeeming and enabling power of our Savior's Atonement every day.

How about Moses, when he was called as prophet to be the mouthpiece of the Lord? His lament is recorded in the Old Testament: "I am not eloquent...but I am slow of speech, and of a slow tongue" (Exodus 4:10). God didn't tell Moses to just have faith, practice his speech, and hang in there, although that certainly could have been an option. Neither did God heal Moses on the spot and solve the problem. Instead He gave him Aaron, a faithful and loyal mission companion who was eloquent with words and strong in speech.

We can't forget Job, who had more than enough to lament about. He lost everything: family, friends, wealth and health. And yet, "In all this Job sinned not, nor charged God foolishly" (Job 1:22). Job suffered an exorbitant amount of loss, heartache, and pain, and the Lord listened to him lament about all of it. That's just the kind of God He is. He loves His children. He knows being a human is hard, and He is always ready and willing to listen when we need to lament. And then He'll help us work through the hard, sometimes offering solutions we didn't know were possible.

You can find many more examples of people in scripture offering up prayers of lament and the Lord's response to their pleading, but the most powerful example was given by the Savior Himself as His suffering in the Garden of Gethsemane was about to commence: "And he was withdrawn from them about a stone's cast, and kneeled down, and prayed, saying, Father, if thou be willing, remove this cup from me: nevertheless not my will, but thine, be done" (Luke 22:41-42). Christ turned to His Father in humility, offered up his complaint, and then affirmed His trust in His Father's will. You know the rest of the story: because of the love of God for all His children, His Only Begotten Son had to suffer, but God did what He could, sending an angel to strengthen him (verse 43). Even with an angel at His side, Jesus was in agony. So He did what we all can do: He continued to turn to His Father and "prayed more earnestly" (verse 44).

Lamenting leads to healing. When Jesus visited His followers on the American continent after His resurrection He invited all of the people to come to Him for help. "Have ye any that are sick among you? Bring them hither. Have ye any that are lame, or blind, or halt, or maimed, or leprous, or that are withered, or that are deaf, or that are afflicted in any manner? Bring them hither and I will heal them, for I have compassion upon you; my bowels are filled with mercy" (3 Nephi 17:7). That is a pretty inclusive list. In the following verse Christ tells the people, "I see that your faith is sufficient that I should heal you." The only thing required on our part is to bring Him our affliction and have the faith and trust that He will help us. That's it. Then allow Jesus to take care of the healing. What a relief and joy it is that He can and will do that for us, just as He did for His followers on the American continent: "All did go forth with their sick...all them that were afflicted in any manner; and he did heal them every one" (3 Nephi 17:9). He didn't leave anyone out. He healed the physically and mentally sick. He healed any who were halt, or in other words, any who were stuck, including those stuck in grief, or any difficult emotion they felt trapped in. He still invites all to come to Him who are afflicted in any manner. No matter the size or type of affliction, the Lord wants you to bring it to Him, and offering a lament prayer is a beautiful way to begin.

Lament prayers aren't just to help when we're grieving the loss of a loved one. Whenever you're experiencing loss of any kind, you can offer up a lament prayer to your Father in Heaven, who is there to hear your complaint. Who better to help than the one who created you? As you humbly turn to the Lord, offer up your complaints, ask for His help, and trust in His answers and timing, He will bless you with guidance and help you find joy in the process.

Questions to Ponder

1. When was the last time you humbly took a complaint to the Lord? Did He help you? How?

2. Is there a complaint you've been holding onto that you could take to the Lord?

Invitation

I invite you to turn to the Lord in faith and offer a lament prayer to Him, either verbally or written. Ask for His help and trust He will help you. If you are struggling to hear His voice, add a fast to your lament.

8

---•---

FINDING JOY IN THE GRATITUDE

"IN EVERY THING GIVE THANKS: FOR THIS IS THE WILL OF GOD IN CHRIST JESUS CONCERNING YOU." 1 THESSALONIANS 5:18

I experienced many blessings throughout my anticipatory months of grief and the months following Baby Kevin's passing. One that stands out most was the godsend of gratitude. To be honest, gratitude wasn't something that came naturally for me when I was younger, in fact, I was kind of a glass-half-empty type of kid. In fourth grade, I went to a friend's home to play one day after school. She showed me her rooms (she had two) and all her cool toys. She even had her own candy drawer, which I thought was the greatest. This friend was an only child and, from my viewpoint, completely spoiled. I remember thinking how cool it would be to have my own drawer filled with candy and wondering why I had to share a room with my sister and didn't get at least one room all to myself. I went home to my five siblings feeling ungrateful and wishing my life were different, even though I had a home filled with love, as well as a whole lot of pretty great things to be grateful for.

I've since wondered whether my friend was wishing for a brother or sister while I was wishing for my own room. Thankfully, during some challenging years as a young adult, I adopted the practice of gratitude. It has become a way of thinking that I embrace. I've never been good at adding to a gratitude list at the end of each day, but I am always looking for things to be grateful for. Somehow, expressing gratitude always helps me feel better. It literally saved me during some of my most difficult days of grieving over my son and, years later, my father.

Four days after we received our son's fatal diagnosis I recorded this in my journal:

> *Yesterday was a good day. The breakdowns were minimal—the ones I did have were brief, and over things that weren't sad, but sweet experiences and feelings letting me know God is aware of me. I've never felt Him and my Savior so near. My sister Natalie has been writing me emails everyday sharing advice and stories about her daughter EmmaLee (who was born with a severe heart defect and DiGeorge Syndrome). My sister Kimmy checks on me every day via text messages. And sisters (I have a lot of them) Meg and Tricia check up*

on me too, as does Mom. I have for sure felt every-one's prayers on our behalf. There has been such an abundance of blessings despite the circumstances with the baby. This has been the most spiritual week of my life. I have this perfect tiny spirit inside me in a flawed little body, and I have my Father in Heaven and my Savior to thank for that.

My first memory of expressing gratitude after Baby Kevin's diagnosis was prompted by all the ultrasound images showing the problems with his brain, heart, and face. I listened to all the statistics and was even offered the option to terminate the pregnancy because my son was "incompatible with life,"[1] as the doctors said. Given his challenges and thinking about all the things that could go wrong in the formation of a body, I was incredibly grateful and humbled to have given birth to seven healthy children. It was miraculous to me. I have never looked at any of them, or any thriving newborn, the same way since. In the days following the diagnosis I praised God in my journal and expressed gratitude for the incredible gift of a healthy body and the miracle of giving birth to seven healthy children.

---

1. https://en.wikipedia.org/wiki/Incompatible_with_life#:~:text=The%20term%20incompatible%20with%20life,considered%20to%20render%20life%20impossible.

I also expressed my gratitude for the gift of having a perfectly imperfect baby boy growing inside me. I vowed to appreciate every moment he was alive within me. I knew – I KNEW – that although his body was broken, his spirit was perfect, and it was a privilege to give him life.

Fast forward to the day of Kevin Jr.'s birth. The day was filled with miserable-joy. Despite everything that initially seemed to go wrong in delivering him hours sooner than anticipated, and without pain medication, I had this to say about the experience in my journal:

> *I've been thinking about how grateful I am that I delivered Baby Kevin natural, with no epidural. I was able to bring him into this world—just me, Heavenly Father, and Kevin supporting me, and with no drugs to dull the experience of giving life to my son. And so grateful I was able to feel good and be fully present with the kids and get up and move around while they were at the hospital. Had I been given the epidural I couldn't have gotten out of bed and I usually feel a little loopy as it wears off.*

Looking at his delivery through the lens of gratitude made all the difference.

The meaning of gratitude is to show or express thanks, as well as an attitude of appreciation under any circumstance—including our darkest, heaviest times of grief. Gratitude is a powerful source of healing on the grief journey and goes a long way in helping you come to a place of acceptance. Gratitude is a fruit of a happy life; it flows easy and naturally when we are happy.

But what about those times we are not happy—the times when we are filled with sorrow and despair? During those times it is important to realize that gratitude is also a seed that can be planted anywhere, anytime, and in any circumstance—especially along your journey of grief. You can plant seeds of gratitude in between the stony paths, all along the up and downhill climbs, as well as alongside the gravely roads. Gratitude has a transformative power for the way we think, the things we say, how we feel, and what we do. It can help bridge the gap between pain and peace, despair and happiness, as well as grief and joy.

There's some interesting science behind gratitude. Robert Emmons, in his book *Gratitude Works*, teaches that gratitude has one of the strongest links to mental well-being.[2] Grief therapist Mary Ricks teaches that up to 30% of your brain shuts down with grief, and it can take a year to eighteen months for it to get back to normal. Seems like gratitude can help manage

---

2. https://www.amazon.com/Gratitude-Works-Creating-E motional-Prosperity/dp/1118131290

that. Gratitude is a protection from destructive impulses of envy, resentment, greed, and bitterness. Emmons shares how people who have adopted the practice of gratitude have better health, are more loving, more forgiving, and closer to God. In his studies he also found that people who keep a gratitude journal are 25% happier.

Gratitude researcher Glen Fox says, "When you experience the feeling of gratitude, your brain releases a combination of dopamine, oxytocin, and endorphins...This is all very similar to a runner's high."[3] Now, I am not a runner, however, I do like to put in my AirPods, turn on some thumpin' music, and bust out a good jog, complete with a few dance moves, on the treadmill. And let me tell you, the high is pretty great. And I have to say, since learning the science of gratitude, I've totally taken advantage of it. Gratitude is my feel-good drug of choice, with zero negative side effects.

The Lord knew the science behind gratitude, which is why I believe He included, "Be grateful"[4] in his list of command-ments. The prophet Alma reminded the people that they were "commanded of God to pray without ceasing, and to give

---

3. https://wenatal.com/blogs/wenatal/the-top-5-reasons-to -practice-gratitude-while-ttc

4. https://speeches.byu.edu/talks/sharon-g-samuelson/grati tude-a-commandment-of-god/

thanks in all things" (Mosiah 26:39). The apostle Paul encouraged the people to "Rejoice evermore. Pray without ceasing. In everything give thanks: for this is the will of God in Christ Jesus concerning you" (1 Thessalonians 5:16-18). Notice how both ancient prophets Alma and Paul mentioned prayer as well as gratitude? God loves it when we include gratitude in our prayers. If we are struggling to see anything to be grateful for, we can offer a prayer of lament, asking Him to show us how and where to plant a seed of gratitude.

About a week before my father's passing I was on "dad duty" for the night, so my mom could get some rest. Dad was miserable. He couldn't stop coughing and his entire body itched terribly, and he was so tired. He just wanted to sleep. I was tired too, mentally and physically. I kept praying (begging actually) that God would grant him relief, but nothing changed. I began to get angry. Then stopped myself. I didn't want to bring that kind of energy into the room. So, I did the only other thing I knew to do. I changed my prayer from asking for help, to expressing gratitude for my father. Immediately, my mind was flooded with beautiful memories of experiences with my dad. I was overcome with peaceful, joy-filled feelings of gratitude for the wonderful father I'd been blessed with. He was more than just my dad; he was one of my most trusted friends. No matter what I was experiencing in my life, I knew I could always go to him for help and support.

Our circumstance that night didn't change. Dad continued to cough and itch and neither of us got much sleep. But those wonderful memories filled me with a measure of peace and joy that helped me get through a really tough night.

Brother David Steindl-Rast, 96 year-old author, scholar, and Benedictine monk, explained it beautifully: "The root of joy is gratefulness...It is not joy that makes us grateful; it is gratitude that makes us joyful...We are never more than one grateful thought from a peaceful heart."[5] When you are feeling overwhelmed and stuck in grief, gratitude can free you. Gratitude can turn you away from darkness, so you can begin to see more light. Gratitude helps to redeem the negative in your life and find the good when it's hard. Gratitude opens your heart to healing, so you can experience a greater measure of joy in the midst of your grief.

Jackson (18), Dakota (14), Emmy (15), Kloe (10), Kevin, Becky, Gracie (7), Janie (3 1/2), Lilly (15 months), and Baby Kevin, shortly after he passed away.

Questions to Ponder

1. What has been your experience with gratitude and grief so far? Have you been able to see the blessings in between your sorrows?

2. When was the last time you experienced the feeling of gratitude? What were you grateful for?

Invitation

I invite you to add one simple practice of gratitude to your morning or evening routine. Notice the way thoughts of gratitude make you feel.

9

— · —

Finding Joy in the Celebrating

"And God saw every thing that he had made, and, behold, it was very good."
Genesis 1:31

My doctor decided to induce labor on May 10th, 2012, which gave me three weeks to prepare for the day I would meet my son. A constant battle raged in my head. I was very excited to meet Baby Kevin, and hopeful God would heal our baby and give me the miracle I wanted. I knew He could do it; I had absolute faith in my Savior's power to heal. But I also knew God's ways are higher than mine, and His plan for my son's life may look different. So I opened my hands and heart to whatever God was about to give us, and did my best to prepare for both possibilities. The doctors were pretty certain that even if our son survived the birth, he wouldn't live long. We might possibly have a few minutes or maybe hours together. My husband and I were concerned about how to help our seven children handle the passing of their brother. We came to the conclusion that we needed to celebrate Baby Kevin's birth day. Whether he lived, or returned to heaven, his birth was a miracle, his life was significant, and he deserved to be celebrated. So we took a birthday cake and candles to the hospital. That decision was possibly the smartest thing Kevin and I have ever done as parents.

Kevin Jr. entered this world at 12:26 p.m. It was clear from the way he looked that he did in fact have Trisomy 13. Contrary to all expectations, he took his first breath, cried for at least 10 minutes, and lived for over an hour. He had fought so hard to live, and we were so proud of him.

Jackson, Emmy, Dakota, Kloe, Gracie, Janie, and Lilly were very excited to meet their baby brother. Each took a turn holding him. They could see how sick he was, and I think it made them love him all the more. There were many tears shed in that hospital room. The entire family felt overwhelmed by miserable-joy, and the grief was heavy as we said our hellos and goodbyes.

Once everyone had their time with Baby Kevin, we brought out the birthday cake and the mood lightened. Ten candles topped the cake, one for each member of our family. We celebrated not only Kevin Jr.'s birth day but also having our entire family together, 19+ years in the making! As Kevin lit the candles, I watched our little Janie's eyes light up. She was only 3½ and had to be woken up from her nap to come to the hospital, so she had been a little confused and out of sorts. Singing happy birthday and blowing out birthday candles made even Janie smile. A sugar rush was never more needed for all of us as we feasted on that cake.

I learned something that day about the power of celebration. I wanted to continue to draw upon that power as our family worked to heal through our grief. The following month we instituted Baby Kevin Night. Instead of celebrating his birth once a year, we celebrated it on the tenth of every month with pizza and ice cream! Sometimes I made homemade pizza with the kids' help; other times we ordered takeout. We always had several flavors of ice cream to choose from, with no limit to how many scoops they could fit in their bowls.

Our pizza and ice cream celebration went on for years on the tenth of every month. We celebrated our son and brother, remembering him and imagining what types of things he was doing in heaven. This simple tradition kept his memory alive. Even when my big kids went off to college, they texted me on the tenth with pictures of them and their roommates celebrating with pizza and ice cream. Our tradition went on regularly for about seven years and sporadically thereafter. I'm grateful for the way it supported us in our grief.

Now you may be thinking, *the last thing I feel like doing is celebrating*—and I get that. But celebrating doesn't have to look like a pizza or ice cream party. There are many ways to celebrate, especially when you consider what the word celebrate means.

I love how Wiktionary.org defines celebration: *To honor in a solemn manner. To honor by rites, by ceremonies of joy and respect. To engage in joyful activity in appreciation of an event.* That word "solemn" is significant. In the Catholic Church, solemnities are the celebrations of greatest importance. Each solemnity begins the night before with an evening prayer. In The Church of Jesus Christ of Latter-day Saints, solemn assemblies are sacred meetings to celebrate holy purposes such as the dedication of temples and sustaining of new Church presidents. "Solemn Assembly" is a phrase from the Hebrew Bible that describes significant gatherings that occurred during Passover and the Feast of Tabernacles. The first temple in Jerusalem was dedicated during the time of a solemn assembly.[1] What better way to remember someone who was such an important part of your life, than by solemnly celebrating them in a holy way.

Another more solemn tradition we have as a family is to visit the temple on or around Baby Kevin's birthday each year. In The Church of Jesus Christ of Latter-day Saints, we serve and worship in holy temples around the world. One of the services we perform is baptisms for our ancestors who didn't have the

---

1. https://newsroom.churchofjesuschrist.org/article/solem n-assembly#:~:text=%E2%80%9CSolemn%20assembly% E2%80%9D%20is%20a%20phrase,ancient%20connection %20with%20temple%20dedication.

opportunity to be baptized into Christ's church. We are baptized vicariously for them, then they can choose whether or not to accept the covenant of baptism. My husband and I were married and sealed as a family to God, Jesus Christ, and the Holy Spirit in one of the Lord's holy temples, making the temple extra special to our family. Serving there helps us feel closer to Baby Kevin. Other solemn traditions might be as simple as lighting a candle for the deceased, writing them a letter, or wearing their favorite color.

God Himself teaches us the importance of taking time to celebrate. In the very first chapter of the Bible He mentioned celebrating seven times. On the first day of creation, God created light, divided the light from the darkness, and at the end of the day He celebrated. "And God saw the light, that it was good" (Genesis 1:4). On the second day of creation, God organized heaven and the earth and at the end of the day, "God saw that it was good" (verse 10). He continued to celebrate at the end of every day leading up to the sixth day when He finished the creation of the earth. "And God saw every thing that he had made, and, behold, it was very good" (verse 31). Notice that God didn't wait until He finished creating the earth to celebrate. He paused to take the time to celebrate every step of the way.

When I was around 22 weeks pregnant, my sister Natalie suggested we choose a song for Baby Kevin. I loved that idea and soon realized I had the words from a children's hymn running on repeat in my head for the past several days. I knew it was the one; that was his song. Through its words, my unborn son shared with us his love for his Savior Jesus Christ. Eleven years later, our family still sings "Baby Kevin's song" at all our important events. Each time we visit his grave we circle around his headstone, holding hands as we sing his song.

To celebrate Baby Kevin's second birthday my husband gifted me a video he created of the day of his birth and graveside service. He included the song, "A Thousand Years."[2] Now every time I watch the video, or hear that song, I celebrate with a smile and a few tears. Music is a beautiful way to remember and celebrate those we have lost. If you are grieving the loss of an older child or adult, consider choosing one of their favorite songs as "their song," to honor them.

A few years after my son died I met a young man named Robert. He was a student in a religion class I was teaching. I arrived to class fifteen minutes early each Sunday morning, but Robert was already there, setting up chairs. Robert was a quiet guy and so kind to everyone. On Thanksgiving day that year, he was crossing a busy street when a drunk driver hit and killed him. As you can imagine, Robert's family and friends were devastated. Several months later I ran into Robert's father and asked how he and his family were doing. His grief was still

---

2. https://youtu.be/iIULIZrUbeE?si=_AnLwz-BcCEOY8q9

heavy as we talked about the pain of losing a son. He mentioned wanting to do something to remember Robert's life, so I shared our birthday and Christmas tradition of going to Kevin Jr.'s grave, having a meal at our family's favorite restaurant before or after the visit, and singing Baby Kevin's song together as a family. The next time I saw Robert's dad, he was excited to share the song they chose for Robert and the traditions they created to help celebrate his life. Finding ways to celebrate helped Robert's family find joy in their suffering.

I think it's significant that on the sixth day God celebrated all His creations, and the following day He created the Sabbath for rest. I think rest, especially when associated with loss, can be a solemn and healing way to celebrate. I love how Elder Dieter F. Uchtdorf taught the importance of rest in his message, "Of Things that Matter Most." He first asked the question, "Have you ever been in an airplane and experienced turbulence?" And then goes on to explain:

> The most common cause of turbulence is a sudden change in air movement causing the aircraft to pitch, yaw, and roll. While planes are built to withstand far greater turbulence than anything you would encounter on a regular flight, it still may be disconcerting to passengers. What do you suppose pilots do when they encounter turbulence? A student pilot may think that increasing

speed is a good strategy because it will get them through the turbulence faster. But that may be the wrong thing to do. Professional pilots understand that there is an optimum turbulence penetration speed that will minimize the negative effects of turbulence. And most of the time that would mean to reduce your speed...Therefore, it is good advice to slow down a little, steady the course, and focus on the essentials when experiencing adverse conditions.[3]

Or in other words, when life gets hard, and especially when your airplane feels like it's going to crash, pull back, slow down, simplify, take care of the basics, and rest. Just as the Lord celebrated His creation with rest, you can celebrate the loss of that person you love and miss so much, by taking a step back and giving yourself permission to rest. In my observations, many who experience loss increase their speed in an effort to escape the grief when the healthier strategy may be to reduce the speed.

I loved everything about having babies. My husband and I deepened our love and commitment to one another with each

---

3. https://www.churchofjesuschrist.org/study/general-conf erence/2010/10/of-things-that-matter-most?lang=eng#p 21

new life we brought into our family. Throughout each pregnancy, having that little human tucked safely inside me brought my soul so much joy. Don't tell my other kids, but Baby Kevin's pregnancy was my favorite. Despite the sorrow I experienced in the anticipation of having to let him go, I enjoyed every moment he was inside me, and I kept my vow not to take one minute of his life for granted. I remember the weeks leading up to his birth. I was really looking forward to meeting him, and I was really sad at the thought of him no longer being with me. I experienced my own personal solemnity as I grieved my beautiful pregnancy coming to an end. During that time I took Elder Uchtdorf's advice by slowing down, focusing on the basics, and resting. I spent hours with my feet up in my recliner. I conserved energy by letting the housework go and setting my own personal record of not showering for a week. I did a lot of praying and pondering. I rocked Baby Kevin and his toddler sisters all together at once – the fifteen-month-old on my right, the 2½-year-old on my left, and Baby Kevin inside me in the middle. In my solemnities the Lord blessed me with some very holy experiences I hold dear to my heart.

Throughout the second half of my pregnancy and after my son died, I took more naps than maybe I ever had before. I gave myself permission to continue slowing down and resting when I needed to. And in a way, I celebrated my courage to feel my feelings (which can be exhausting, but worth the effort) and to show up for my family, especially when I didn't feel like it. The

Sabbath also provides an opportunity to draw strength from celebration on the day set apart for the Lord; why not include Him in your celebrations? He loves your person too, knows them better than anyone else, and is taking good care of them now. If you aren't sure how to celebrate, ask the Lord to help you find ways to best honor your loved one. He will help you find ways that will be just what you need, when you need it.

The Lord can also help you celebrate the progress you're making on your grief journey. It's easy to measure the gap between where you are now and the happy, peaceful feeling you long for. But the Lord wants to help you see and celebrate your gain today, no matter how small your progress. Maybe a week ago you couldn't get out of bed, but today you got up and took a shower before climbing back into bed. Or maybe yesterday you "ate your feelings" with junk food, but today you began your day with a banana. Those are gains worth celebrating. Celebrate the gain, don't focus on the gap, and give yourself the grace to grieve, trusting that the Lord can help you see your progress and what you can do to take the tiniest step forward. He's cheering you on, my friend, and He loves you so much.

Speaking of junk food and bananas: if it isn't already obvious, food is one of my favorite ways to celebrate. We buried our son in a beautiful little cemetery in Malad, Idaho, about two hours from our home in Utah. I was born in Malad, my mother grew up there, and her father (Grandpa Moon) was still living there on his cattle ranch when Baby Kevin passed away. Several other family members are buried there, now including both Grandma and Grandpa Moon. Their infant son Boyd, who passed away a few hours after birth, is also buried there. Before Baby Kevin was born Grandpa Moon offered us the other half of Boyd's adult size grave. At first I resisted, thinking I wanted him buried close to our home. But as time went on, I warmed up to the idea. I especially loved thinking of him resting near so many family members.

The morning of Baby Kevin's graveside service, we gathered at the mortuary. His casket was placed in the back of our suburban and we caravaned the two hours to the Malad cemetery with our parents, siblings, nieces, and nephews. We celebrated Baby Kevin – our son, brother, grandson, and cousin – with a simple graveside service which included prayer, scripture, music, words, balloons, hugs, and tears—lots and lots of tears. Then we drove the three minutes from the cemetery to downtown Malad where the servers at our favorite restaurant, the Dude Ranch, were waiting for us. We sat together at one long table and filled our stomachs with lots of comfort food, ranging from French dip sandwiches to turkey dinners, with ice cream for dessert. We talked, even laughed, and found solace in good food and being together. We found joy in the celebrating.

I think God knew what He was doing when He created human bodies with the need for food. Our bodies need continual sustenance. We eat multiple times a day to nourish our mind, body, and soul. The need for food gives us the chance to slow down, pause, and give the Lord a word of thanks. And for our family that day, that meal helped us find comfort and joy in celebrating the life of Baby Kevin.

There's no right or wrong way to celebrate your loved one. God celebrated with observation and praise. We celebrated with pizza, ice cream, a cake, and candles. Some celebrate with a visit to the cemetery and flowers. Last Memorial Day weekend we visited my father's grave with a picnic dinner and Snickers (his favorite) for dessert. Others celebrate birthdays and death days with a party or by doing something they loved to do together when their loved one was alive. My dad loved puzzles. He was born on New Year's Eve, so every year my mom, his kids, and grandkids celebrate his birthday and the new year by doing puzzles. I think every one of us has memories of putting together puzzles with Papa Tom. Throughout New Year's Day we text each other pictures of puzzles we're working on. It's so fun to remember and celebrate Dad by doing something he loved, as well as connecting as a family.

I think sometimes we make the mistake of avoiding celebration because we're feeling guilty, angry, or sad . Maybe we don't feel worthy of happiness, especially when we believe the death of a loved one was premature. Some people think that celebrations or remembrances only make the grief worse. Others feel the best way to move forward is by not talking about their loved one and removing any reminders of them. This may bring relief initially, but limits our ability to process through the grief. Unprocessed grief will keep you stuck.

We can also mistakenly believe the only celebration will be in the next life, when we see our loved one again—which simply isn't true. I agree that the reunion with those we've loved and lost will be the greatest of all celebrations, but in the meantime, we can have more frequent celebrations, even solemn ones, all along our path of grief. God created us to have joy, even in the most painful and difficult life experiences. In order to have joy we have to be intentional in looking for opportunities to create it. Celebrating the life of our loved one is a beautiful way to create more joy in our lives. And be sure to celebrate the progress you're making each day on your grief journey too.

Questions to Ponder

1. What are some ways you remember and celebrate the life of your loved one who's passed away?

2. When was the last time you celebrated them?

3. When was the last time you celebrated how far you've come on your grief journey?

Invitation

I invite you to think about the things you used to enjoy doing with your loved one. Think about the things they loved in life. Then create one simple way to celebrate their life and make time to carry it out within the next week or two.

10

---·---

YOUR GUIDE

"I WILL IMPART UNTO YOU OF MY SPIRIT, WHICH SHALL ENLIGHTEN YOUR MIND, WHICH SHALL FILL YOUR SOUL WITH JOY." DOCTRINE & COVENANTS 11:13

E very year my husband and I attend an event called Education Week, held at Brigham Young University. The campus is tucked up against the beautiful Wasatch Mountains in Provo, Utah. For four days we take classes on a variety of subjects, including, education, religion, personal development, parenting, communication, and more. There are hundreds of classes to choose from and one particular year I went to several classes taught by a grief therapist named Mary Ricks. I was beginning my Grief Coaching practice and wanted to learn from Mary, who had years of professional training and experience, and was well acquainted with grief from her own personal losses.

For about an hour each day of the conference, Mary taught me about grief. Parts of her presentation included how to grieve in order to continue moving through the grief journey in a healthy, healing way. I was intrigued to learn that in my experiences of losing my son and father, I had done all the "hows". I had checked all the boxes. I'd assembled a group of people to help and who I felt safe talking to. I journaled my experience through grief. I had (and still do) celebrated my son and my father. I engaged in a cause to honor my son, and so on. I left Education Week with a question that continued to be on my mind throughout the months that followed, *How did I know to do all of those things—How did I instinctively know how to grieve?*.

The answer to my question surfaced seven months later at a Grief Conference held on the same campus. This time I was attending as a presenter, where I taught about the grief cycle, and also sat on a panel focused on how to help children grieve.[1] For two days I was immersed in the grief world and there was a moment between classes where I felt Christ answer my question as these words came into my mind. "It was My Spirit who taught you how to grieve".

Of course, who better to teach me about grief than my elder brother Jesus, who had already suffered in the Garden of Gethsemane for all my pains and sorrows. And who better to guide

---

1. https://www.churchofjesuschrist.org/bc/content/shared/content/images/magazines/ensign/2018/03/march-2018-ensign-magazine-mormon_2046508.pdf

me through my grief journey than the one who knew how to suffer because He had suffered all things. In fact, not only did he guide me in my grief, but he also helped my husband and I see how to help our children work through their grief in the most beautiful, personal, and unique ways.

I have a firm belief in the principles I teach throughout the grief cycle. I have found they work best when you let the Savior and His Spirit be your guide. I invite you, if you haven't already, to surrender your experience with grief over to the Lord and let go of all expectations for how you, or others think you should be grieving. The Savior can teach you how to apply these principles to your precise needs in very personal ways. I have given you the "whys" for mourning, lamenting, being thankful, and celebrating. I've also supplied a few ideas for "what" you can do and "how" you can do it. It's up to you to figure out the specific "whats" and "hows" that will best help you work through the pain of your loss. As you include the Savior, He'll give you the personalized help, direction, and answers you need. I pray you find hope and healing as you take courage and embrace the grief cycle with Jesus Christ, so you can create a joy-filled life, filled with what matters most.

Brigham Young University Life After Loss Conference
March 2023

Questions to Ponder

1. Think about others whose grief you have been privileged to witness. What have they done that you want to avoid? What have they done that you want to emulate?

2. How did you expect to grieve? How is it different from how you are actually grieving?

3. Have other people placed expectations upon you for

how they think you should grieve? What would it feel like to let go of all of those expectations and grieve in your own way?

Invitation

I invite you to let go of all the expectations around how to grieve that aren't serving you: both the expectations you've created personally and the ones created for you by others. As you learn about the grief cycle, use your agency to choose ways to mourn, lament, be grateful, and celebrate. Invite your Savior into the process and co-create your grief journey with Him.

11

— · —

Your Capacity for Joy

"And oh, what joy, and what marvelous light I did behold; yea, my soul was filled with joy as exceeding as was my pain!" Alma 36:20

My oldest son Jackson was about to start kindergarten at Rosecrest Elementary. He and I were sitting in the hall outside his classroom and we were next in line for his assessment. I overheard his teacher ask another student, "Can you give me some examples of opposites?". My mind raced, wondering if our preschool co-op had taught Jackson and his friends about opposites. I turned to him and quickly asked, "Jax, do you know what opposites are?" He shook his head with a questioning look. I proceeded to give him a sixty-second lesson on opposites. Listing examples seemed easier than trying to define the word. Light and dark. Day and night. Happy and sad. Good and bad. He caught on immediately, and when his teacher asked him the same question, he nailed it.

While explaining opposites to my five-year-old all those years ago, I didn't realize how much power an opposite holds. Everything has an opposite. Newton's third law of physics states, "Everything exists with its equal and opposite," meaning that you cannot exist in one state without the potential of going to the other. This is especially true when it comes to emotions. Whatever negative emotion you feel, your capacity to experience the opposite is also available. This is really good news when you consider that the deeper your soul is pierced with sorrow, misery, or despair, the more space you have to experience feelings of joy, peace, and hope. If you were to rate your sorrow on a scale of 1 to 10, with 10 being the most painful, your capacity for joy becomes a match to that same number, with 10 being the most joyful. Living in the grief cycle gives you access to the solace and joy your soul longs for.

Since the loss of our son, I have seen Newton's third law of physics working repeatedly in my life. Because of the depth of my loss and heartache, my capacity for joy has grown exponentially. I've also learned that the more I turn to the Lord, opening my heart and hands to receiving His help, the more frequently joy shows up in my life.

My journals are filled with joyful experiences. The entry written on May 9, 2016 about visiting Baby Kevin's grave to celebrate his fourth birthday, is one of my favorites:

> *My weekend was the best! It seems that every*
> *year in May, since Baby Kevin's passing, some-*
> *thing special happens. I found out Saturday, at his*

grave, that I'm going to be a grandma!! Jax and Aubrey gave me a Mother' Day gift with two Big Hunk candy bars (my favorite) and two positive pregnancy tests. I screamed, jumped up and down, and my daughter Emmy got it all on tape. It was the best!

That day holds one of my favorite memories, packed with so much joy. Our loving Father in Heaven knows that the only way to experience the big and beautiful joys of this life – the joys we were born for – is to experience the opposites in the same measure. No sorrow, grief, or pain would mean no joy, happiness, or peace. That sounds like a world no one would want to live in.

Alma the Younger taught what he knew about opposites as he explained how deeply he suffered because of his sins, and then the equal measure of joy he felt after he came to Christ for help and to repent. "Yea, I say unto you, my son, that there could be nothing so exquisite and so bitter as were my pains. Yea, and again I say unto you, my son, that on the other hand, there can be nothing so exquisite and sweet as was my joy" (Alma 36:21). There is a valuable lesson to be learned from Alma's experience. In order for him to access the opposite of his sufferings, he had to bring Christ into the equation.

Just as Alma needed his Savior to help him change, we also need our Savior's help. He has the power to heal all our losses.

Christ Himself encourages us to pray for help to access the opposites of our sorrows: "If thou art sorrowful, call on the Lord thy God with supplication, that your souls may be joyful" (Doctrine & Covenants 136:29).

If you are struggling to experience the level of joy your suffering has qualified you for, then turn to the Savior, embrace the grief cycle, and allow Him into every facet of your grief. Those practices might be the missing link.

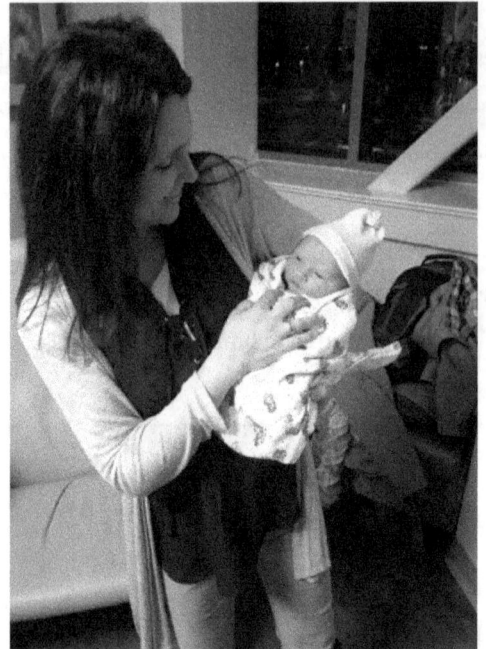

Grandma Becky holding Beau, her first grandchild.

Questions to Ponder

1. On a scale of 1 to 10, what level of sorrow have you experienced on your journey of grief? Describe the sorrow you've felt.

2. On a scale of 1 to 10, what level of joy have you experienced on your journey of grief? Describe the joy you've felt.

3. Has it been your experience that sorrow and joy are related?

Invitation

I invite you to pray for joy and believe you can have it. Pray the Lord will send you the joy you desire and that you can be open to receiving it.

12

---•---

THE BEST IS YET TO COME

"WHEN YOU ARE COMPELLED TO GIVE UP SOMETHING OR WHEN THINGS THAT ARE DEAR TO YOU ARE WITHDRAWN FROM YOU, KNOW THAT THIS IS YOUR LESSON TO BE LEARNED RIGHT NOW. BUT KNOW ALSO THAT AS YOU ARE LEARNING THIS LESSON, GOD WANTS TO GIVE YOU SOMETHING BETTER". – F. ENZIO BUSCHE

Mother's Day came three days after Kevin Jr.'s passing. My family showered me with birthday wishes, cards, hugs, and breakfast in bed. Kevin spoiled me with a delicious steak dinner. But the very best part of the day was waking up to Janie, our 3½-year-old, snuggled up next to us. She was having a conversation with her dad about her little brother. She said with confidence, "Jesus is going to fix Baby Kevin's lip." Our son had a bilateral cleft lip and palate and our little two-year-old knew Jesus could take care of that. Jesus will also take care of every single part of his body that was broken. One day Baby Kevin's chromosomes will be repaired and I'll have a beautiful perfect baby boy to raise. My little Janie's words filled me with hope and peace, but my current reality was that my arms were empty. I was sad, heartbroken, and missing my baby.

Several days later I found myself looking out over the beautiful, peaceful cemetery where we'd just laid our son to rest. The days leading up to his graveside service were a blur. I'm convinced we are given abilities beyond our own to plan and execute all the funeral arrangements. It's a lot, don't you think? On top of your grieving you've got decisions to make, things to plan and organize—often in a matter of only a few days. I'm convinced the only way we survive is by our brain going into some level of shock, so we can wade our way through without shutting down completely.

Driving away from Malad, I breathed a huge sigh of sadness as I watched the cemetery getting smaller and smaller. It was as if all the emotions I had felt throughout my anticipatory grief before Baby Kevin was born came rushing back to join the mass of emotions I was trying to sort through since his passing. Tears streamed down my cheeks and my heart felt incredibly heavy with sorrow. The thought of the days ahead, with no baby to care for, was too much to bear. And yet, within the sadness, I can't deny the gratitude I felt for my many blessings over the past five months. Never in my life had my Savior been so near. He truly did walk with me and, at times, carried me through my grief. Despite the sorrow that was my current reality, I had hope that things would get better and that I would be okay. I trusted in the prophet Ether's words: "Whoso believeth in God might with surety hope for a better world" (Ether 12:4). I clung to the belief that, over time, my world would get better.

As I have interviewed women like me who have endured the loss of a child, I have noticed a pattern. Those who have walked the long and winding road of grief with their Savior Jesus Christ are at peace, work hard at living life in the present, and find deep joy in their day-to-day living. They continue to grieve in varying ways, but haven't become completely lost in their grief. They live big, full, joy-filled lives in whatever circumstance they are in. When I ask these mothers, "If you could go back in time and your loss be erased, as if it never happened, would you do it?" Their answer is almost always, "No, I wouldn't." Someone who has never known the daily blessings of the enabling and redeeming power of the Atonement of Jesus Christ may believe it impossible to feel that way. Some might think these women are crazy, but the power our Savior has to heal our pains and re-deem our losses cannot be understood until experienced. Jesus Christ's power enables us to become stronger, wiser, happier, more peaceful, higher versions of who we were before our loss. We become yoked to Christ as He sanctifies us through our experience in the most intimate and beautiful ways, forever changing us going forward.

A few days before Baby Kevin was born, I recorded these thoughts in my journal:

*I'm scheduled to be induced on May 9th at 10
p.m., so most likely little Kevin's birthday will be
May 10th—a great day for a birthday! That day
will be a wonderful day, no matter the outcome...I
hope he will live long enough for us to get to know
him and him to know us...I believe this little boy
has lessons for our family and those around us, and
those lessons will take time for us to learn. But if
not, if he's only with us a few minutes, hours, or
days, I'll be grateful for every second, and trust
that God is in charge of every detail.*

If you are seeing no hope and no light, I invite you to turn
to Jesus Christ and trust Him. My cousin Nikki has been a
beautiful example to me of unconditional trust in her Savior.
She lost her three-year-old son Tui in a tragic accident. During
some of her darkest hours of grief, she held onto the hope that
things could and would get better. She knew life had more joy
in store for her, and that the joy would eventually come.

Jesus gives Martha a beautiful promise: "Said I not unto thee,
that, if thou wouldest believe, thou shouldest see the glory of
God?" (John 11:40). It seems as though he's saying to Martha
and each of us, *Remember how I told you, you just need to
hang on, have faith, and believe that everything will be made
right?* We can trust in the promise given by the Lord in Isaiah
51:11: "Therefore the redeemed of the Lord shall return, and

come with singing unto Zion; and everlasting joy shall be upon their head: they shall obtain gladness and joy; and sorrow and mourning shall flee away." Such a beautiful promise.

I know this to be true with all my heart, because Jesus always keeps His promises.

Wise advice was given to one of the ghosts in the *Haunted Mansion* movie, who, for years, couldn't find peace: "Grief unprocessed, will keep a spirit stuck." Also great advice for the living. As you embrace the grief cycle as a way to process your grief you'll be able to rise above and beyond it. As you live within the grief cycle, you can find joy and meaning in your loss as you wait for the Lord's glorious Second Coming, when the graves will be opened (Matthew 27:52-56) and we will be reunited with our loved ones again.

Another promise I hold dear is the word of the Lord that the prophet Alma shared with his son concerning death. "Now my son, here is somewhat more I would say unto thee; for I perceive that thy mind is worried...The soul shall be restored to the body, and the body to the soul; yea, and every limb and joint shall be restored to its body; yea, even a hair of the head shall not be lost; but all things shall be restored to their proper and perfect frame" (Alma 40:1, 23). That promise brings me such peace as I trust that my father's broken body from cancer and our son's broken body from defective chromosomes will both be restored to perfection. Everything, through Christ, will be made right. Such a beautiful promise.

I know this to be true with all my heart, because Jesus always keeps His promises.

I was disappointed we didn't have more time with Baby Kevin, but incredibly grateful for every moment he was with us. He taught each of us such beautiful lessons and, even today from the other side of the veil, he continues to teach us what it means to truly love someone, the worth of a soul, and the Lord's love for each of His children. We are all better humans because of Kevin Jr.'s influence on our family.

Life is wonderful and beautiful, even amidst all the hard. It continues to get better, and I believe the best is yet to come. I love the words of Elder Jeffery R. Holland: "Faith is always pointed towards the future. Faith builds on the past but never longs to stay there. Faith trusts that God has great things in store for each of us and that Christ truly is the High Priest of good things to come."[1]

Jesus Christ can teach you, as no one else can, how to access the peace that comes from accepting what is. He can help you to believe all things work together for your good (Romans 8:28). And, if you'll allow Him to, He will step in and take over so you can let go of what you can't control. He will show you how to

---

1. https://speeches.byu.edu/talks/jeffrey-r-holland/rememb er-lots-wife/

mourn, lament, be grateful, and celebrate, so you can find joy in the things that matter most.

I know this to be true with all my heart, because Jesus has always kept His promises to me.

Hang in there my friend. Keep going, keep believing. The best is yet to come.

Acknowledgements

Writing my first book, Too Perfect for This Life, *took years. I knew very little about writing and publishing but I felt I had a story worth telling.*

Writing Finding Joy in The Grief Cycle *was a very different experience. It only took six months to write, thanks to the earthly angels God sent me.*

So many thanks to all of you who came to me in your grief and courageously shared your stories with a stranger. Your humility and vulnerability inspired me to write this book.

A very special thanks to all who joined my very first Finding Joy in the Grief Cycle *book club. Your input was invaluable.*

Amanda Frances, thank you for showing me the clear path to publishing as many books as I want to write.

Robin Sharma, thanks for teaching me how to structure my time so that writing became consistent and easy.

To my wonderful editor, Marci McPhee, thank you for being a wizard with words, knowing all the rules (and when to break them), keeping me in check, your encouragement, and becoming so invested in my work. You are an answer to prayer and now that I don't need to worry about grammar and rules, writing is so much more fun!

Thank you June, for your copyedits. And thanks Aunt Jeri, for your attention to detail and catching the things we missed.

And thank you, Jesus, for teaching me about the beauty and blessings of grief and all the gifts of joy that can be found, even in the midst of it.

CONNECT WITH BECKY

Becky was born in Malad, Idaho, and has lived in the Salt Lake Valley most of her life. She married her high school sweetheart Kevin, and together they have eight children.

Becky graduated from Utah State University with a bachelor of science in elementary education and currently teaches high school seminary part time. She founded the blog, *What Matters Most* in 2008 (kevinbeckyfam.blogspot.com), where she journals about her love for God, family, and living the gospel of Jesus Christ.

Becky is a Certified Creation Coach with an emphasis on grief coaching. Her online coaching program, *Joy in the Mourning,* helps grieving mothers find peace and healing through Christ as they navigate their grief journey.

Becky believes everything we experience in this life has purpose, and that a loving and all-knowing God works all things for our good. Her deep faith and trust in her Father in Heaven and His Son Jesus Christ guides all that she does.

Becky loves spending time with her family, being a homemaker, planning vacations, listening to audiobooks while working on a project, and going to lunch with a good friend.

To learn more about Becky and Baby Kevin's story, read her memoir, *Too Perfect for This Life*, available on Amazon[1].

Looking for more support on your grief journey? Scan the QR code or visit:

www.whatmatterswithbeckybeck.com

---

1. https://www.amazon.com/Too-Perfect-This-Life-grieving/dp/B0BW2CNK39

If this book has been helpful to you in any way I invite you to leave me a review on Amazon or Goodreads, so more of our grieving friends can access the joy that can be found in the grief cycle.

ALSO BY BECKY BECK

HERE'S A GLIMPSE OF BECKY'S MEMOIR

Prologue

The Phone Call

It was Monday January 2nd, 2012. I can still picture myself sitting on the floor of our bedroom. We had just gotten home from a week-long visit with my brother Rob's family in Arizona. My husband Kevin was with me and we were both completely exhausted from driving straight through the night. I was trying to muster up the energy to unpack, when my cell phone rang. I didn't recognize the number, but assumed it was Fetal Fotos calling to remind me of my appointment for the next day. It was a follow up from our initial ultrasound on December 24 at eighteen weeks pregnant. The technician wasn't able to completely confirm the baby's gender, so she wanted us to return a week or two later.

When I answered the phone, a girl from Fetal Fotos was on the other end of the line, however, she wasn't calling to confirm the second appointment. "Our doctor reviewed your ultrasound, and he found a problem with the baby's head. He recommends you contact your doctor for an ultrasound."

"Oh, well, several of my babies have had big heads; they run in the family," I responded.

"No...," she hesitated, "It's not actually the head, but the face. It's the width of the face that isn't right." I thanked her for the information and hung up the phone. I repeated the conversation to Kevin; we were both confused, but quickly convinced ourselves it was just a precaution. We agreed to wait for the ultrasound with my midwife later that week before jumping to any conclusions.

Continue reading on Amazon.com[1]

Scan QR code to read *Too Perfect for This Life* on Kindle or purchase a paperback on Amazon.com

---

1. https://a.co/d/hgRJ16o

Coming Soon

Scan QR code to get on the wait list and be the first to know when *Embracing Your Seasons of Grief* is available

BY BECKY BECK

www.ingramcontent.com/pod-product-compliance
Lightning Source LLC
Chambersburg PA
CBHW070721130626
46553CB00005B/2094

* 9 7 9 8 9 8 7 8 0 4 5 2 0 *